Monetary, Fiscal and Trade Policies Series

CHALLENGES OF THE POST-COMMUNIST FINANCIAL-CURRENCY POLICY

MONETARY, FISCAL AND TRADE POLICIES SERIES

Trade Policy in A Globalizing World
Yuki Watanabe and Haruto Yamashita
2009 ISBN: 978-1-60456-830-1

U.S. Trade with Developing Countries: Policy, Programs and Trends
Kalan R. Geisler
2009 ISBN: 978-1-60741-122-2

Measuring the Economy: GDP and NIPAs
Kemal Sahin
2009 ISBN: 978-1-60741-199-4

Taxation, Tax Policies and Income Taxes
Warren J. Berube and Camron N. Pinto
2009 ISBN: 978-1-60741-626-5

Challenges of the Post-Communist Financial-Currency Policy
Avtandil Silagadse and Micheil Tokmazishvili
2009. ISBN: 978-1-60741-150-5

Monetary, Fiscal and Trade Policies Series

CHALLENGES OF THE POST-COMMUNIST FINANCIAL-CURRENCY POLICY

AVTANDIL SILAGADSE
AND
MICHEIL TOKMAZISHVILI

Nova Science Publishers, Inc.
New York

For permission to use material from this book please contact us:
Telephone 631-231-7269; Fax 631-231-8175
Web Site: http://www.novapublishers.com

LIBRARY OF CONGRESS CATALOGING-IN-PUBLICATION DATA
Available upon request
ISBN: 978-1-60741-150-5

Published by Nova Science Publishers, Inc. ✝ New York

CONTENTS

PREFACE

The given work represents a review of the problems of transformation as well as the results of implementation of the Financial-currency policy in the post-communist countries. It contains characteristics of alternative circumstances of implementation of the financial policy and the conclusions on their possible transformation. It gives a review of the impediments existing in the exchange rate regulations of different countries and the results obtained in the course of nearest experience are also illuminated.

The given work is targeted at reviewing the subtleties of the transformational development projected to the foreign currency risks. Paramount importance is attributed to those exchange rate regimes, which have become a major catalyst of economic development in a number of countries.

The study is intended to define a). Likelihood of rise of currency policy challenges now in the base of experience of the financial crisis of the 90s in the post communist countries and b). Exchange regime options that are rationale for the countries.

Keywords: post-communist countries, transformation, financial crisis, foreign exchange policy.

About the Authors

Avtandil Silagadze*

Professor, Doctor of Economics, Member of the National Academy of Georgia. He was vice-rector of Javakhishvili Tbilisi State University, Dean of Faculty of Economics, Member of government of Georgia, Parliamentarian.

Micheil Tokmazishvili†

Doctor of Economics, Member of the Council of the National Bank of Georgia, Senior researcher of the Foundation Case-Transcaucasus. He was the head of the Department of Macroeconomics of the Budget office of the Parliament of Georgia, the country manager of the program of the Economic Development Institute of the World Bank in Georgia.

* Correspondence to: Mobile Phone: (+995 99) 54-42-42, E-mail: avtosilagadze@mail.ru

† Correspondence to: Tel/Fax: (+995 32) 442-566; mob: (+995 95) 270-276, E-mail: m_tokmazishvili@yahoo.com

INTRODUCTION

Economic development of the post-communist countries in modern times represents rather complex ways of economic transformation. In this we mean not the final goal of the transformation (that is putting economy on the market wheels), but rather the process of changes (sometimes experimental in character) which hardly provided any significant progress in the stable development of our national industrial production.

The changes which began in the 90s were followed by the financial crisis. It's true that later on, the crisis was overcome, but the transformation programs (starting with the concept of the Washington Consensus, as well as the programs for combating poverty and the plans of strategic development) proved unable to ensure swift development of the former Soviet countries and failed to prevent the financial crisis.

During the post-communist period, the strategic vectors of economic transformation of the said countries were mostly based on the expectations for evolutionary development and gradual adaptation with the market rules which commanded relatively less sacrifice, although under the influence of different political as well as economic and institutional factors, the economy fell into the market shock which in its turn, required radical changes, but on the other hand, these changes proved not equally effective at all stages of the development.

Successful implementation of the strategic programs was always accompanied by the side-effects which popped out at each stage of the development and required trans-active expenditures. The economic knowledge existing in the transformational countries was no more capable of defining the whole spectrum of the expected changes and, therefore, the development of economic life under an unexpected scenario instigated a certain test for the government.

The expert scholars of the transformational economy give a different assessment to such phenomena. On the transitional phase, the new economic thinking collided with the old, stereotype mode of reasoning. The transformation process was a historical stage which revealed the mistake that had been made.

The given work is targeted at reviewing the subtleties of the transformational development projected to the foreign currency risks. Paramount importance is attributed to those exchange rate regimes which have become a major catalyst of economic development in a number of countries. The study intends to define a). the likelihood of rise of currency policy challenges at the present time in the base of experience of the financial crisis of the 90s in the post-communist countries and b). exchange regime options that are rationale for the countries.

Chapter 1

THE CONCEPTS OF TRANSFORMATION

1.1. THEORETICAL BACKGROUND OF TRANSFORMATION

In the post-communist countries, in the initial stage of the social-economic changes, two ways of economic transformation were defined: first – evolutionary and second – the so-called "shock"; both of these notions were based on the trivial philosophic postulates of evolutionary and revolutionary alterations. *

In compliance with the environment existing throughout different post-communist countries, both ways were considered to be acceptable. A considerable part of the social-political forces supported gradual transition to the market economy, although in the beginning of the 90s, the economy of the transitional countries found itself in a shocking situation indeed, and this required implementation of radical changes, especially in the monetary sphere.

The transformation policy relied upon two theoretical directions:

1. Mainstreaming based on the neoclassical economy which implies a generalized approach to all countries. It acknowledges similar problems in all countries and allows implementation of transformation by way of liberalization, stabilization and structural changes; in fact, this is a concept supporting the "shocking therapy".

---

* The renowned economist V. Leontiev compared adaptation to the market economy with teaching little children how to swim: a child may learn swimming in a long period of time but under the circumstances that are not endangering his/her life and also in another case, when the child is thrown into water and in an extreme situation, at the expense of a great risk to life, he/she yet manages to survive.

2. The second direction is based on the principle of institutionalism and the post- Keynesian approach. According to this idea, the countries differ from each other and their programs have to be also different in compliance with the environment and the existing conditions. The "third way of democracy", which is different from the market socialism, should be formed in the mentioned countries (Lavigue M., 2000, p.17).

The first direction was lobbied by the International Monetary Fund (IMF – Stanley Fisher and his followers) and another one was taken by the World Bank (WB, Joseph Stiglitz and his followers). As it was revealed later, neither of them was free from mistakes. Different results were yielded by the reforms which had been implemented under different time-limits and resources. The reforms undertaken by the IMF were mostly founded on the neoclassical principles. Liberalization, stabilization and the structural transformation were broadly promoted, although some claimed to favor the institutional direction that emerged every now and then. Consequently, the obtained results revealed the differences in transformation of the countries in transition.

This direction in transformation of the economy envisaged the following:

1. Economic liberalization which implied: liberalization of prices, canceling the state control over the enterprises and a free foreign trade; transfer of the state property to private hands by way of privatization.
2. Macroeconomic stabilization, which had to be realized by means of regulation of the monetary mass and reform of the credit issuing institutions.

As a result of the transformation, the production resources would move from the low-production enterprises to the ones that would be capable of utilizing them and would attract new resources as well. In addition, state interference in their operation should be ruled out.

Numerous old enterprises were destined to be born dead. The reforms in the financial system were based on formation of the new banking structure, which developed across the post-communist countries via the western ways. The Central Bank was mainly engaged in undertaking emission whereas the numerous commercial banks were busy with issuing credits. Monetary regulation, restricting inflation and bank supervision were defined as the functions of the Central Bank.[†]

[†] Some countries (such as Estonia, Lithuania and Latvia) objected to implementation of the monetary policy; they introduced the systems similar to the currency boards and adjusted the national

The experts emphasized the rate and speed of the reforms. One of them was supporters of shocks and others were supporters of gradual expansion of economic reforms. Their points of view were equivalent to the above-mentioned evolutionary and shock theoretical directions. Moreover, there were so-called followers of a "third way", requiring step-by-step gradual approaches to the transformation to the market economy. Supporters of gradual directions, as their critics noted, required political guaranties as well as tight financial support particularly from the IMF to perform the reforms, but later they supported the "Washington consensus" conception, which implied an orthodox scenario of shocking therapy (Papava, V., 2005a).

The policy of the "shock therapy" undertaken on the basis of generalized transformation approaches enabled the countries to embark on the road of swift development. The transformation was preconditioned by the macro and micro-economic circumstances. This kind of policy was quickly realized in connection with only the liberalization of trade and the prices as well as with regard to holding back inflation and privatization of minor enterprises but it took much longer to implement the reforms in the financial sphere. In addition, the regimes (looking rather ambiguous even today) emerged in this sphere, which are creating barriers in the way of financial stabilization of those countries (Fisher and Sahay, 2000).

It is worse to mention that some politics of shock therapy (e.g. Gaidar, in Russia) in the present day institutional changes in post-communist countries are considered a priority and counted as a new stage of development. Efficiency of founding market institutions and the extent of performed economic policy are recognized as one of the lessons learned from the earlier period of transition (Gaidar, 2004).

1.2. PECULIARITIES OF TRANSFORMATION

The post-communist countries, not compared with other countries, happened to make a shift towards the private ownership in entirely different historic, cultural-institutional conditions and under very uncommon production experience as well, but (unlike other countries) the transactional anguish of transformation and the crisis situations felt especially painful to the post-Soviet countries. Escape

currency to the currency of some other foreign country under a fixed exchange rate. Thus the orientation on integration with those countries which would serve as donors and major investors was ensured from already the initial stage.

from the economic crisis implied implementation of the measures which would ensure the growth of pure investments.

It's true that during the transformation period the former Soviet countries were experiencing similar problems with the Central European countries, yet it turned out that those countries were totally different despite their similarity in public management that had been unanimously practiced there throughout the very recent historic past. The results of implementation of similar transformation programs turned out to be different across those countries. The newly emerged viewpoints maintained that the changes were still in development and the structural transformation had to be continued further (Stiglitz, 1977). Such approaches justify the completeness of the theoretical concepts of transformation but the mistakes were caused by the actions of concrete governments.

On the initial stage of transformation certain differences were revealed among the countries. All countries had different starting positions in the beginning of building their economy because they started enhancing development by employing various means. In effect, two groups of the countries have been formed: the first, where the macroeconomic stabilization was comparatively successful (the countries of Central and Eastern Europe, as well as the Baltic countries) and the second, where the success seemed less tangible (the post-Soviet countries).

The budget deficit, inflation and different monetary regimes which failed to provide security with regard to escaping the monetary crisis, became a major characteristic feature for the post-Soviet countries. It is just the monetary crisis that is typical to the 90s which affected Russia especially in the years 1997–1998 and caused a ripple reaction all across the post-Soviet area. The financial crisis had especially negative influence on the above-mentioned countries, and the main reason for this was the weak development of the financial institutions there.

The currency and banking crisis became a feature for the post-Soviet countries which is a clear indication that the financial system there is based specifically on the weak development of these two institutions and underdeveloped banking system as well as on the problems in the state regulation. An effect of the crisis of the 90s was that industrial production in the post-Soviet countries was reduced 2.2 times compared to the countries of Central and Eastern Europe and the Baltic countries as well.[‡] In addition, if the recession period in the European countries amounted to 4 years on average, in the post-Soviet countries this indicator reached 7 years (see table 1).

Table 1. Transitional Recession (fall) and the Great Depression

The countries	duration of recession (The years)	decrease of cumulative production (%)	real GDP 2000 (1990=100)
The countries of Central and Eastern Europe, the Baltic countries	4	23	107
Albania	3	33	110
Bulgaria	4	16	81
Croatia	4	36	87
The Czech Republic	3	12	99
Estonia	5	35	85
Hungary	5	15	109
Latvia	6	51	61
Lithuania	5	44	67
Poland	2	6	144
Romania	3	21	82
Slovakia	4	23	105
Sloveni	3	14	120
The post-Soviet countries	7	51	63
Armenia	4	63	67
Azerbaijan	6	60	55
Byelorussia	6	35	88
Georgia	5	78	29
Kazakhstan	6	41	90
Kyrgyzstan	6	50	66
Moldova	7	63	35
Russia	7	40	64
Tajikistan	7	50	48
Ukraine	10	59	43
Uzbekistan	6	18	95
The Great Depression, 1930-34			
France	3	11	-
Germany	3	16	-
The United Kingdom	2	6	-
The USA	4	27	-

The source: World Bank (2002a).

Stabilization and the structural reforms of the 90s yielded positive results in the countries of Central Europe as well as in the Baltic countries and speeded up

‡ In this respect, Georgia was attributed the "highest grade". The production decreased to 78% in 1990, this indicator being three times higher than that of the USA during the times of great depression

the pace of growth. The mentioned countries managed to react against the foreign financial-monetary shocks and succeeded in escaping this situation with the least amount of losses. Already by the year 2000 most of them reached the level of 1989 and even surpassed it, whereas the second group of countries (post-Soviet) proved to be considerably slow in forming the financial institutions; they also failed to achieve stabilization, and the structural reforms were implemented only halfway. The mentioned countries are still pretty backward compared to the 1989 level.

Table 2. Dynamics of the GDP in the post-Soviet countries, per capita (USD)

	2000	2001	2002	2003	2004	2005	2006
Azerbaijan	647	697	758	880	1045	1586	2362
Byelorussia	1036	1235	1467	1801	2350	3084	3792
Estonia	4108	4544	5385	7093	8638	10230	12007
Latvia	3293	3520	3972	4802	5944	6969	8781
Lithuania	3260	3487	4076	5373	6543	7494	8592
Moldova	311	362	412	498	662	771	876
Russia	1762	2088	2364	2967	4089	5310	6877
Georgia	648	690	736	875	1135	1433	1746
Armenia	620	691	779	924	1182	1625	2128
Tajikistan	139	173	193	243	321	353	424
Turkmenistan	1327	1199	1083	1017	979	973	923
Ukraine	2287	1836	1372	1052	883	785	640
Uzbekistan	598	517	458	393	388	371	557
Kazakhstan	1223	1486	1650	2055	2856	3756	5043
Kyrgyzstan	277	305	317	376	429	473	536
Average total	1435,7	1522,0	1668,1	2023,3	2496,3	3014,2	3685,6

The source: The UN statistic database.

Among all post-Communist countries there were only a number of countries (mostly the Baltic countries) which succeeded in escaping the low level of development and increased the wellbeing of the population to a significant level (see table 2). Their GDP is 2.5 times higher than similar indicators in other countries. Only the pace of economic growth of the oil-producing countries was accelerated by means of income generated from the natural resources. In other countries there is still a relatively slow tempo of economic growth which is caused by the slow institutional changes going on there (see table 3).

Table 3. The pace of growth of the GDP in the post-Soviet countries

	2000	2001	2002	2003	2004	2005	2006
Azerbaijan	11.1	9.9	10.6	11.2	10.2	26.4	34.5
Byelorussia	5.8	4.7	5.1	7.1	11.4	9.4	9.9
Estonia	7.9	7.7	8.1	7.1	8.1	10.5	10.9
Latvia	6.9	8.1	6.5	7.2	8.7	10.6	11.9
Lithuania	4.1	6.6	6.9	10.3	7.3	7.6	7.8
Moldova	2.1	6.1	7.8	6.6	7.4	7.5	4.1
Russia	10.1	5.1	4.7	7.3	7.1	6.4	6.7
Georgia	1.8	4.8	5.5	11.1	6.3	9.6	9.1
Armenia	5.9	9.6	13.2	14.1	21.5	21.2	16.9
Tajikistan	8.3	9.6	10.8	11.1	10.3	6.7	7.1
Turkmenistan	5.5	4.3	0.3	3.3	5.1	9.1	9.1
Ukraine	5.9	9.2	5.2	9.6	12.1	2.7	7.1
Uzbekistan	4.1	4.3	4.2	4.5	7.7	7.1	9.1
Kazakhstan	9.8	13.5	9.8	9.3	9.6	9.7	10.6
Kyrgyzstan	-5.2	5.3	0.1	7.1	7.1	-0.2	2.7
Average total	5.6	7.3	6.6	8.5	9.3	9.6	10.5
Average total for the Baltic countries	6.3	7.5	7.2	8.2	8.0	9.6	10.2
Average total for other countries (without Baltic and oil & gas exporting countries)	3.6	6.7	6.5	8.9	10.5	8.0	8.3
Average total for the oil & gas exporting countries (Russia, Azerbaijan, Kazakhstan, Turkmenistan)	9.1	8.2	6.4	7.8	8.0	12.9	15.2

The source: The UN statistic database.

By the end of the 90s, dwelling on different levels of development the World Bank undertook grouping of the countries and eventually, the two groups were identified: Central Europe and the Baltic countries on one hand, and South-East Europe together with the post-Soviet countries on the other (World Bank, 2002). In the first group of countries, by the year 2000 all of them (except for the Czech Republic) managed to achieve the GDP level of 1990. The acute macroeconomic crisis had blocked not only once the economic growth in Bulgaria and Romania and this was caused by insufficient structural reforms. The real GDP in 12 countries of the former Soviet Union reached the level of 1990 only by 62.7%.

Nowadays, the countries are being grouped under a totally different principle. In fact, the group of countries related with the European Union in the membership format has already been recognized; another group is composed of the countries that are in the neighboring regime and the last one among them is Russia. This kind of division is undertaken on the basis of a political feature. The post-Soviet countries and the countries of central and east Europe are operating under the geographic feature, whereas the developed countries of the European Union and the former Soviet Republics (except for the Baltic countries) are distinguished by the characteristic economic feature.

Today, in the former Soviet countries economy is still backward compared with the level of development of the Central European states. Among different transformational concepts and programs existing currently, the motivation of joining the European Union proved to be the most viable and effective; this is the stimulus which has established clear cut objectives before the countries which have decided to embark on this route. Accordingly, the transition period will gradually become the possession of the past because the course is firmly taken towards the European Union and its neighbor policy. All countries of central and East Europe and a greater part of the post-Soviet states (except for Russia) are involved in this integration process. In addition, obstacles caused by the financial institutions were automatically overcome by the members as well as the candidate countries of the EU by means of the policy targeted at joining the monetary zone of the European Union, but in a number of countries this problem is still pending for further resolution.

Now, the post-communist countries are called the “new market countries” or the “newly emerged market countries” (Lavigue, M., 2000, p.16). This notion implies free movement of the capital and giving opportunities to the international funds for uninterrupted operation across the territories of the above said countries. From this standpoint, attributing the name of newly emerged markets to the countries in transition is completely proper and justified. It is notable that enhancing free movement of the capital and establishing relevant financial institutions in this regard has become major compass in political development of these countries and it played a dominant role in forming their present-day standing as well.

The question concerning future directions which these countries are going to follow is still on the agenda. Accordingly, the attitude to the transitional stage has changed and the name: “countries in transition” was also changed into a different qualification label which is: “underdeveloped countries”, while the post-communist countries of Central and Eastern Europe were given the name of the “newly emerged market countries”; now they are either the EU member countries or the candidates for membership.

Thus, the approach has changed according to different characteristic features that the post-communist countries adopted unlike the development trends in other countries. Differentiation of the countries was undertaken despite the fact that at the starting point of the market transformation all these countries had a common institutional base in the form of the state economy.

Inflation

In the post-Communist countries, at the initial stage of liberalization of the prices inflation and hyperinflation became an issue of the day; the living standards decreased rapidly, distribution of profits turned uneven in character and unemployment reached its climax.

The first results of transformation proved particularly vulnerable to the population; the government turned unable to escape the shock situation by choosing the proper course which would ensure the growth of pure investments necessary for the stable development of the economic transformation process. This enhanced inflation which later on was followed by hyperinflation (see table 4).

Table 4. Inflation Dynamics in the post-Soviet countries (%)

	1990-95 in average	1996-2000 in average	2001-2006 in average
Armenia	1685,4	8,3	3.1
Azerbaijan	705,2	3,2	11.4
Georgia	3310,6	14,6	6.3
Kyrgyzstan	324,4	24,1	4
Moldova	432	22,7	10.5
Tajikistan	738,2	122	11
Uzbekistan	527,7	41,6	14.7
For 7 countries in average	1103,4	33,8	8.7
Russia	536	39,4	12.8
The post-Soviet countries	1028,4	56,7	9.2

The Source: World economic Outlook Database. (2007).

It is clear, that all the countries found themselves in an "open space" and the free market developments created certain risks which in the existing immature financial situation played the role of a hindering factor, which manifested itself in blocking the industrial production and slowing down the pace of wellbeing on one hand, and facilitated development of inflation on the other. Because of the lack of experience in managing or avoiding the said risks, they tended to be more and more realistic.

In fact, liberalization of the prices enhanced growth of deficit in the solvency balance because the competitive goods were non-existent in the country. Allowing a free exchange rate of the currency caused sharp devaluation and increase of prices on the imported goods. In addition, in effect of the lack of the capital, the interest rates increased and the growth of capital investments was considerably hindered.

In the 90s, because of the financial crisis and growth of inflation, economic development plunged in recession. Based on the neoclassic postulates the mainstream school recognized this, yet only in part and still asserted that worsening of wellbeing was only arbitrary and measuring it was of relative character. Adherents of the institutional trend recognized that the poverty rate particularly increased throughout the post-Soviet countries; it instigated the strongest social shock which was caused by negligence of the peculiarities of the economy of those countries.

The countries of East Europe, South Caucasus and Central Asia started the transformation process since the times when they had one of the lowest indicators in the world with regard to the Gini coefficient. In 1988 only one person out of 2.5 was qualified as living below the absolute poverty rate with less than 2.15 dollars of income per day. In ten years the number of such people already amounted to 1 out of 5 persons. 68% of the Tajik population lived in absolute poverty, - 50% in Kyrgyzstan, - 40% in Armenia and - 42% in Georgia. Now, from the point of view of disproportion, the post-Soviet countries are attributed to the highest ranking countries in the world; this can be explained by the spread of corruption and disregard of the “market rules of the game”.

The neo-classical direction recognized that stabilization of inflation was followed by real GDP. Therefore, it was stabilization that first took place and afterwards it was followed by the growth, yet the question about the inflation threshold, which then would enhance economic growth, was answered in different ways. Today, the answer to that question is relatively concrete and is connected with the EU requirements: the countries have to reach the average inflation indicator which is less than 3%.

The Financial System

On the first stage of transformation great attention was paid to transformation of the Central Bank and formation of the effective fiscal system, although the problems emerged in a number of countries with regard to corruption. Because of weakness of the public institutions economic development proved to be a failure. In fact, it was revealed that formation of the financial institutions should be a necessary driving force of transformation. Building the financial institutions turned to be the sphere which was assessed differently by the neoclassicists the institutionalists; the latter attributed paramount importance to establishing public as well as market institutions which had to be built gradually and not in a spontaneous manner.

With this regard, in the post-Soviet countries, the government had only two alternative policies: **1. Restrictive monetary policy**, which is targeted to mitigating the inflation by way of introducing certain restrictions on money supply and interest rate and 2. **Expansion monetary policy,** which is aiming at investments in private production and decrease of unemployment by the money supply.[§]

Of these alternatives, the post-Communist countries adopted the first one and meanwhile, the individual efforts and interaction of the free market forces were ignored, although later on, it turned out that in fact, such attitude equaled to neglecting economic stimulus and other incentives.

Moreover, as far as the main problem was state debt growth, money supply and " open market" operations were stimulating inflation growth.

General agreement among the economists exists only in two cases. It is recognized that the strict monetary manipulations are only justified when: 1.The demand is high because of the growth of the monetary mass and 2. The growth of consumption versus production is neutralized by improving the demand-supply system and by ensuring supply-orientated policy

Implementation of a restrictive monetary policy will not yield anti-inflation results but it will take place only in case when the demand is stable or tends to decrease, whereas the local production becomes uncompetitive and the import is growing.

In the post-Soviet countries, expansion monetary policy was implemented together with liberalization of economy, which in fact, along with the growth of inflation preconditioned growth of inflation as well (see Figure 1).

[§] In the literature of post-communist countries, it is named as "strict" and "liberal financial-credit policies"

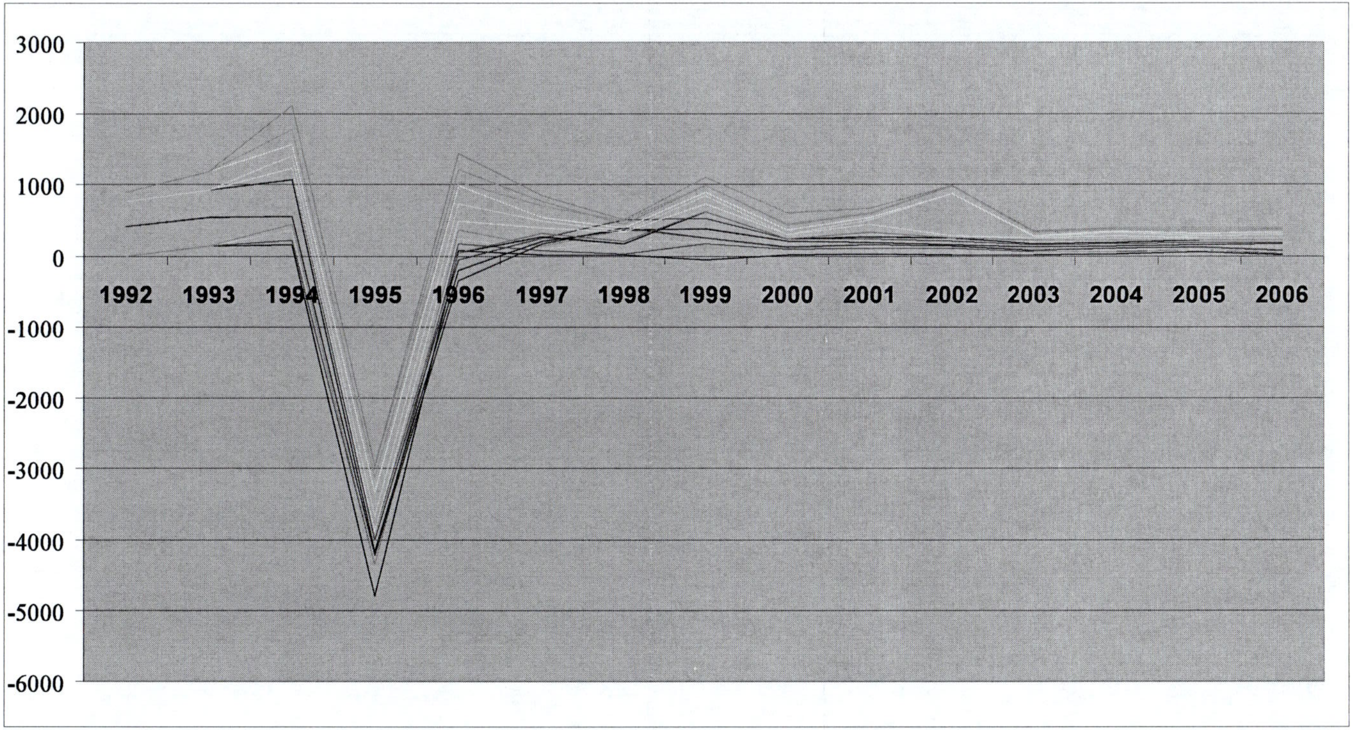

The Source: EBRD

Figure 1. Inter-relevancy (%) of inflation (average annual) and broad money (M3) in the post-communist countries

Now, it is possible to understand why the growth of monetary mass may cause inflation (liberal monetary policy). It is not at all doubtful that the growth of the monetary mass will bring about increase of prices, since no structural changes had been carried out in the public enterprises because of the "soft budget restrictions". Overwhelming majority of the public enterprises were working in the monopoly conditions. Therefore, they were authorized to change the prices according to their own disposition. Along with this, they established fictitious trade relations with other companies at the background of non-existent effective state or market control upon their economic activities. In this case, money growth caused not the abundant demand which might influence the increase of production but brought about inflation of the supply.

A question comes to floor whether the control imposed upon the growth of the money mass could hold back increase of inflation. It is less likely that the enterprisers would change the style of their work because of the monetary control exercised in the conditions of state owned property, for in fact, they delivered the product by taking the other way round the financial system and mutual financing was the common practice they were engaged in; this is what enabled them to increase the prices. In order to improve the said situation reorganization of the functional and management systems of the public enterprises had to be undertaken, which because of the negative features characteristic to the public property proved unable to yield any real economic effect. Yet, as a result of privatization, financial mediation turned out to be significant but weakness of these institutions blocked the way to production practiced by means of relevant financial resources and this in turn, caused increase of the supply inflation.

The empirical data prove that the greatest influence over the production can be attributed to the money channels. It is mostly carried out through the change of the monetary mass which causes different results:

1. Increase of monetary mass has an impact on decrease of the interest rates which causes growth of investments and expansion of production on the whole;
2. By means of increase of the monetary mass the bank deposits will grow which will have a positive impact on issuing the credits and allocating investments. Giving credits to the banks becomes important in cases when the countries are targeting at disposing the money. This means that the change of the monetary mass is in line with the definite goals that the country is pursuing;
3. In effect of increase of the monetary mass the prices grow on the financial assets and the securities. As a result of the growth of the prices

on the assets, capitalization will increase whereas the risks will go low and the credits and issuance will increase.

4. Increase of the monetary mass will cause growth of the financial assets which are in the ownership of the households. In particular, income on the assets saved by them is increasing and along with this, the amount of products produced by those households is also growing. The effect of change of the assets that are in the ownership of the households depends on how and in what way increase of the income of the population will be manifested. If it causes increase of the consumption of the imported goods, then the pace of the economic growth will be slowed down.
5. The monetary mass tends to change together with the changes of the exchange rate. Increase of the monetary mass is restricted in the conditions of the fixed exchange rate, because in such a system the interest rates are endogenous. The channels of the exchange rate are only operative in the conditions of exchange rates that are floating freely and when the interest rates are reflected in the exchange rate and are manifested in the trade relations as well. The exchange rate channel can make an impact only when targeting inflation becomes the main feature. In a long lapse of time the exchange rate is defined by the fundamental factors such as parity of the consumption capability whereas during a short period of time it is connected with the balance of the financial assets. In such cases increase of the monetary mass will reduce the interest rates in effect of which the exchange rate of the national currency will go down, but meanwhile, pure export and issuance will grow.

Thus, five transmission mechanisms are used during implementation the monetary-currency policy: the interest rates and mechanisms of giving credits to the banks, money channels, the household assets and the exchange rate mechanisms. As a result of increasing money supply (1) price of the interest rates, the exchange rates or the price of the financial assets gets changed (2). Afterwards, this kind of changes will influence utilization of the investments and the pure export as well (3) and finally, all the above said will cause the changes in the production process (4). The countries are different from each other by the profundity of these phases, dynamics and their significance.

The situation with regard to the state expenditures will also influence the mentioned dynamics. As soon as the monetary mass becomes the cause of the growth of the investments, it will be reflected positively on the economic development, but if increase of the monetary mass occurs in parallel to raising the state expenditures then positive effect of the economic growth will be neutralized.

In the post-Soviet countries, the monetary mass had an influence on the production process by means of the exchange rate (by the change of the value of the national currency in particular). Other mechanisms were underdeveloped and the foreign currency was widely used to protect the produced goods.

It should be emphasized that the value of the national currency expressed in the foreign currency and its value, which is estimated by the domestic calculations with regard to the consumer prices, are different from each other. It means that the national currency which is exchangeable on the foreign currency is not compatible with the price of this money because the foreign currency has turned into a remedy for protecting the money from inflation and for making monetary savings.

In the post-communist states, import results in profits for the producer countries which later on, can be used for purchasing raw materials (also the privatization facilities, land etc.) at a low price at the local markets. In such cases, the exchange rate of the national currency reflected the inflation expectations and had nothing to do with the rate, by means of which balance in export-import would be achieved. Yet the free prices, on the other hand, proved unable to stimulate development of the local production and weakness of the financial institutions and their little share in mediation was destined to fail with regard to ensuring stable economic growth and progressive development. In effect of this, the financial risks were increased and the threats of financial crisis also occurred.

1.3. Forming the New Institutional Relations

Due to different historic conditions, in the post-Soviet, Eastern and Central European countries different institutional environment was formed. These conditions are interpreted in different ways. The neoclassicists are putting emphasis over the macroeconomic conditions whereas the institutionalists are underlining the longevity of the communist regimes. This is why, because of the paternal mentality with regard to the state, building of the market institutions proved to be much more difficult in the post-communist countries.

Considerable decrease of the role of the government was a generalized precondition for the transformation of the post-communist countries. Obviously, economic functions of the state had to be decreased; yet without the state, the spontaneous emergence of neither of the institutions would be completely satisfactory. By the end of the 90s the World Bank changed its attitude and started to talk about the role of the state in the countries of transition (World development Report, 1997).

According to the assertions of the neoclassic school, the state should deliver the authority of forming the relevant institutes to the market and it should be reinforced by the banking, tax and other legislative documents. In addition, the contribution of the state expenditures in the GDP should be reduced.

Under the requirement of the institutional school, building of the market institutes should be undertaken by the state, but in what sphere: in service, in production or where? This question is still pending for the answer because the swift liberalization and reduction of the tariffs left the countries unprotected from the affect of the shocks inflicted by the foreign markets. This tendency revealed itself most strongly in the financial crisis. The newly created financial institutions proved unable to survive the foreign shocks and in fact, they destroyed the economy one more time. Certain part of the economists demanded protection of industrial production on the transitional phase. This was emphasized in the post-communist literature not only once. The use of Neokeinzian policy was considered rational, although this kind of recommendations reinforced the discrepancies with the neoclassic school.

Transition enhanced forming of the standard market economy, although, according to the claims of the neoclassicists, in some countries, in Russia for instance, the new "mutants" of public management were created.

As practices affirm it, the policy of stabilization projected to market is not automatically followed by the process of economic growth. I. Shumpeter wrote about the so called "creative destruction": the society first is being destroyed quite rationally and it is only afterwards that the process of goal-orientated creation starts. He meant formation of a favorable social-economic environment in this process. The "creative destruction" never happened in the post-Soviet countries; it acquired a chaotic form and in fact, destruction of absolutely everything took place. This, in its turn, enhanced appearance of such phenomena as "momentary speculation", "black markets" and "illicit enterprising".

In the post-Soviet countries, forming of the markets was carried out under the combined actions of the spontaneous forces and because the existing social-political and institutional conditions hardly allowed operation of the spontaneous forces, the market institutions were also formed by the public investments and were managed by means of the "stop and go" principle.

Transformation of a social-economic system rejects practicing of any single universal program per se. It represents a unity of local and progressive measures well framed in time; it also requires implementation of the actions corrected by way of everyday changes and commands to envisage the specific results. With this regard, not a single economic program had been perfect. They never took in view the local results and also, neglected the changes and deviations that had been caused by each remedy and which might have happened in the course of implementation of these programs. Therefore, they only reflected the opportunities for changes in ideal and general contours. Successful implementation of the programs (dwelling on both positive and negative economic consequences) is only possible if they are based upon the useful historical conclusions as well as the resources and experience existing in the country.

Major weakness of the economic transformation is also preconditioned by the fact that the "shock therapy" which in fact, was a "hard blow" on the economy, required substitution of the owners of the property in any case (whether there was enough capital for accumulation and investment or not).

The basis of the economic programs is that implementation of individual interests should increase economic welfare thus ensuring higher life standards for the entire society. Such a context should be created through the efforts of relevant institutions of the market forces and then implemented by means of political undertakings, which only should be an additional remedy.

It mustn't be disputable at all that the social-economic system of each country ignores utilization of any universal prescription or a program. Despite its international significance, it commands implementation of local and perspective planning as well as filtration and correction which should be undertaken in the prism of everyday changes, with proper time and space in view. From this standpoint, the countries which have embarked on the road of transformation should make a choice between stabilization and implementation of active social policies, between providing credits and investments for the economy and unemployment, between tax and investment policies, etc.

An active state and the spontaneous market forces represent the generating forces of the economy of the countries in transition, when the state is trying to regulate its economy by way of denationalizing the property and activating the monetary instruments, whereas the market forces are still in the process of acquiring the due shape. The latter are unable to generate enough incentives for the economic revival and command for implementation of active investment plans, through rationalization of foreign exchange policy, which in turn, is restricted by the low export potentials of enterprises and payment balance deficit.

Eventually, some questions which arise with regard to transformation, especially when the transformational countries will be able to catch up with Western Europe, mainstreaming gives the following answer: liberalization, openness and the anti-inflation policy enhances development of the economy, but in the post-Soviet countries, transformation was started from the lowest level of development and therefore, the future scenario can be rather pessimistic (UNECE, 2000).

Chapter 2

THE LESSONS OF THE FINANCIAL-CURRENCY CRISIS

2.1. FINANCIAL CRISES AND THEIR DEVELOPMENT

There is no precise definition of "financial crisis" in the literature, but a common view is that financial crises are caused by some misbalance in the economy which has a negative impact on its growth. The fall of the assets and bankruptcy of the commercial structures is a characteristic feature of this process. The crises emerge from the financial and economic violations on which the economy has a rather acute reaction.

A financial crisis is preceded by the delay of the capital flow and a sharp decrease of the import volumes. In such conditions, aspiration of the owners of the bank deposits to the national currency becomes stronger, because its power tends to be dependent on the standing of the international reserves. The stronger the dependency on the mentioned reserves during the pre-crisis period, the more dramatic is the aftermath of the crisis: the national currency is undergoing greater devaluation and the escape from the crisis proves to be more costly. Normally, the coefficient of dependency on the international reserves starts growing two years earlier than the crisis. All the efforts of the government not to allow a sharp correction of the exchange rate and to strengthen the national currency and its fixed rate often prove to be incompatible with the economic abilities; it yields a counter-reaction with regard to development of exports and the monetary policy acquires an expansive character; this process is also accompanied by the rise of the volume of domestic credits. It is true that generally, the fixed exchange rate is considered to be the main indicator of the investors' faith in the stability of the internal financial system, but a few months before the crisis, this faith easily disappears giving rise to the financial agitation which expedites the appearance of the financial crisis even more.

Normally, there exist three main types of financial crisis: the currency, bank and debt crisis:

1. The **currency crisis** emerges as soon as the national currency gets devaluated. In such cases the government, in order to protect the national currency, is obliged to spend a certain amount of the international reserves and undertake the currency interventions at the stock exchange markets; another option is to increase the interest rates. Emergence of the crisis is always preceded by a peaceful period which may last almost two years prior to it. In that period the real value of the currency is rather high but three months prior to the crisis, the real value of the real exchange rate of the currency goes down. Re-assessment of the value of the national currency decreases even after the crisis had reached its climax.

   Changes in real exchange rate are different in the industrial and developed countries and they cause the decrease of the reserves, the currency "disaster", and other negative effects depending on the characteristic features of each country.

   The currency crises are preceded by worsening of the situation in the trade sphere which is the first symptom of the expected crisis and plays the role of the barometer in heralding such negative proceedings.

   Two years prior to the crisis, inflation keeps growing but approximately one year earlier, inflation becomes moderate. Presumably, inflation turns out to be a real result of the policy carried out by the government with regard to maintaining the exchange rate of the national currency. During the 12–18 months after the commencement of the crisis, the inflation rate keeps growing, yet later on, it gradually goes down again.
2. During the **Bank crisis** the banks loose a part of their assets or they go bankrupt, the bank balances get worse and the share of the immovable credits tends to grow in the bank portfolios. In the times of the bank crisis, mass withdrawal of the bank deposits are traceable but in the industrial countries with developed economies (for instance: by the end of the 80s in Finland, Sweden and Norway) the bank crisis was not associated with the mass withdrawal of deposits, but in the countries with a transitional economy, this process develops with rather vulnerable consequences;

3. The **Foreign debt** crisis reflects the situation when the state is no longer in a position of serving its internal as well as foreign debts and liabilities.

There are correlative links among the mentioned types of the financial crises although these crises are conducted through different scenarios.

During the modern period, the currency crisis is the most wide-spread phenomenon. More than 160 cases of the currency crisis have been reported throughout the world and one third of them happen to develop in the countries in transition. Its average duration (or in other words, in the times when the pace of the GDP growth reaches the level of the pre-crisis period) amounts to 1.6 years. The developed countries escape the crisis faster than the developing countries.

One of the results yielded by the currency crisis is the currency disaster. It means the fall of the national currency rate down to 25% or even lower. This period tends to last even longer than the crisis itself, and its average duration amounts to 2.0 years.

Currency crisis is tightly connected with the banking crisis, which is often an accompanying factor to it. The bank crisis, although rather rare in occurrence than the currency crisis, is the longest and the most disastrous to the country's economy.* In general, escaping the bank crisis commands more financial resources in the developing countries than in the developed ones.

More than 50 cases of the bank crisis have been acknowledged and the overwhelming majority of them occurred in the developing countries. In the aftermath of the bank crisis, the developed countries need at least 4 years on average in order to restore the pre-crisis level whereas the developing countries need only 2.8 years. It is true that the developing countries need less time for rehabilitating the economy, but on average, the losses of their production are greater compared to those of the developed countries.

In the times of the bank crisis industrial production, in fact, decreases to 14–15% whereas during the currency crisis this indicator amounts to only 5–7%. It may happen sometimes, that the production losses are not preceded by such crises and they only make corrections in the exchange rate.

In the course of comparing countries, it becomes clear that in the developing countries, the bank and currency crises occur less often than in the developing countries and the reason for this is the fact that these types of crises may have similar conditions of origin or one crisis may bring about another; the countries may experience the bank and currency crises at one and the same time as well. Normally, the bank crises come prior to the currency crises but sometimes, the crises emerge simultaneously overlapping each other. In particular cases, the currency crisis happens prior to the bank crisis.

The currency, bank and debt crises existed simultaneously in 1994–95 in Mexico and in 1997 in Eastern Asia. The bank crises preceded the currency crises especially in the developing countries, in Turkey and Venezuela in 1994-95. The bank crises preceded the debt crises in Argentina and Chile in 1981–82. Contrary events also took place in 1997, in the East Asia countries, especially in Indonesia, when the currency crisis turned into the bank and debt crises.

It is hardly possible to conclude from the above statements that the fact of one crisis being prior to another is necessarily based on the causal links between them, although it is equally impossible to exclude such an option either. The development of the crises and their proceedings in each country are always preconditioned by the special circumstances currently going on in the given countries.

Financial instability is a precondition for the occurrence of the crises which then go round a chained circle: in effect of the growth of the interest rates investments go down, thus hindering the economic growth. In parallel to that, the enterprising risks also keep growing, which makes the balance situation in the banks rather critical, hence making the expectations for the crises even more acute. Increase of the interest rates, failure of the financial deals and the expectations for the currency devaluation are destroying the non-financial institutions and making the bank problems quite acute. In effect of the decrease of the amount of investments, credits, as well as of economic activity, the banks start panicking and this is followed by transfer of the national currency into the foreign one; this will precondition increase of the interest rates.

In the countries with inflation, the loans are issued for a long period of time, the interest rates are fixed for a certain period and inflation is under control; in them, devaluation of the national currency causes no wide-scale expectations of inflation and the exchange rate keeps moderate as well. In the mentioned countries, increase of the interest rates fails to influence the movement of the capital flows because the credits had been issued on long-term conditions.

The situation is different in the countries where the inflation rate is rather high, and the bank credit is issued on a short-term basis. Decrease of inflation does not have enough influence either on the economic progress or on the investment growth and this happens because of the expectation for an unexpected

* For example, the expenditure undertaken for the purpose of escaping the bank crisis in Chile and Argentina in the beginning of the 80s, reached 40% of the GDP, whereas the immovable credits in Malaysia in 1988 and in Shree-Lanka in the beginning of the 90s exceeded 30% of overall credits

devaluation of the national currency. Since there is a serious fear of such an expectation, the credits are issued only for a short period of time.

In the current period, the situation is different in the post-Soviet countries and the average inflation amounts to 8–16%, although they also have common basis with regard to considerably limited credit resources and restricted enterprising environment. Despite the fact that inflation expectations are scarce, the credit movements are not protected from certain risks which creates a precondition for the speculative blows on the currency situation.

As soon as the currency situation gets the first speculative blow, the Central Bank, in order to protect the national currency, will be given an opportunity for the following option: either to sell the international reserves or increase the interest rates. When the profits increase, then the banking system will grow alert and when the investors feel that the Central Bank is in position of increasing the interest rate, they start attacking the currency in order to get profits by way of selling it. In such conditions, mostly because of existence of the short-term credits and accumulation of large-scale debts in foreign currency (which is happening at the background of the feeling of ambiguity and confusion), the currency crisis gets matured and this, in its turn, becomes a precondition of the financial crisis.

Thus, our conclusions can be that the currency crisis appears in cases when a serious danger of speculative attack against the national currency emerges. Unlike the above said, appearance of the banking crisis is preceded by the problems in conversion and the actions of intervention undertaken by the government, but the times of heavy crisis are also accompanied by systematic crisis in balance of payment as well; during such times, structural problems emerge and the international reserves decrease, which in its turn lays foundation to appearance of the currency crisis.

The elements of currency, banking and debt as well as the tax crises may exist simultaneously, because to some extent, they are connected by similar reasons and results, yet such a link, as it was mentioned above, is hardly always possible. Worsening of the situation in the banking sector is not necessarily effective to inflict a currency disaster. Currency disaster may be the result of the situation at the financial markets. It influences the macro and micro economic development of the country and is rather sensitive to the foreign economic factors as well as to the political developments and therefore, the currency crisis is a milestone of all categories of the financial crisis; it cannot be brought down to only the change of the exchange rate, because change of the exchange regime does not always mean existence of the problems in the currency rate. Change of the regime of the exchange rate does not always cause aggravation of the banking, inflation or tax problems either.

2.2. Problems of Defining the Currency Crisis

Historically, there are two definitions of the currency crisis: first – in narrow understanding, it is associated with the Monetary School and is connected with the bank panic; second – it is connected with the cost of the assets, failure of the activities of the financial and non-financial institutions, as well as with deflation and malfunction of the markets.

In the economic literature, different indicators are considered to be the crisis criteria: decrease of the national currency to 25% versus the USD and 10% devaluation compared to the previous year; negative change of the pure capital flows (assets) amounting to at least 5% in correlation with the GDP; decrease of the pace of GDP and devaluation; leakage of the reserves and the nominal deflation; change of correlation of the reserve losses against the money supply; 1.5 points deviation in correlation to M1 of the average index changes of the exchange rate as well as of the interest rates and reserves; change of the exchange regime and devaluation (Dabrowski, M. ed., 2001, p.14-15).

Definition of the crisis is especially popular in the mass media, which sounds like loss of certain profits in a country. In addition to this, according to the viewpoint of the overwhelming majority, the main indicator of the crisis is the decrease of the international reserves (correlation of M3 with the international reserves). In economic theory the following other criteria are recognized as indicators: standing of the bank systems, level of the international liquidity (a short-term foreign loan in correlation with the reserves) etc. Everything depends on the principles according to which the currency crisis can be defined.

The level of international liquidity is the simplest indicator of the crises. This is the ability of the Central Bank and the economy to withstand the provisional changes of the capital flows, so that they would not influence the macro-economic results (for instance, the exchange rate and the GDP). It is rather difficult to express the influence of these changes in quantities. For example, evaluation of the international reserves (correlation of the reserves with the 3 months import).

The crisis becomes a fixed fact as soon as it reaches its final phase and manifests itself in ultimate devaluation of the currency or in certain losses of a real sector in case the government manages to defend itself from the speculative attacks of the agents and will not allow the currency to yield to devaluation. Generally, it is impossible to define the crisis by means of a single definition. It has an arbitrary character and can be brought down to different indicators which are expressing reduction of the currency exchange rate, radical correctives in the macroeconomic policy, leakage of the foreign capital and investments, loss of the agents' belief in the national currency and their speculative attack against the exchange rate.†

According to all the above given criteria, change of the currency exchange rate is a real indicator of the currency risks. Deviation from its course or its decrease for a long period of time compared to the existing stable course should be considered as the first symptom of commencement of the crisis (The same idea is developed in: Tomczynka, M., 2000, p. 8).

During the fixed currency regime, decrease of the international reserves and the changes of currency rate under the conditions of the free floating exchange ragime are the indicators of commencement of the crisis. Despite this, alarming indicators of the crisis still turn unable to forecast the crisis but can reveal the problems, that the government should be aware of, in order to take prevention measures in due time.

In all countries, each episode of the crisis is particularly peculiar and it is impossible to reflect all its dimensions in a qualitative way. They don't tend to develop under similar scenario and this hardly allows the opportunity of their generalization. It is most important that the crisis often develops unexpectedly, and therefore, it is impossible that the prognosis made with regard to the crisis and based on one particular model or empiric research can be successful. Thus, the system of the crisis indicators can not be defined to the final extent.

The system of indicators which reflects expectations of the crisis comprises the dynamics of the international reserves and the currency changes as well as the real exchange rate, the credit environment, inflation, deficit of the state budget and the trade balance, deficit of the current account, correlation of the monetary aggregate M3 with the international reserves, real growth of GDP, interest rates, fiscal deficit etc. In general, the weak economic situation in the country serves as good "nourishment media" to the crises.

Dwelling on the peculiarities of the development of the countries, it turns necessary to draft a unity of specific indicators for all countries and diagnose them. In addition, it should also be considered that the crises are not only manifestation of the economic problems, but worsening of the political situation and the changes of subjective influence of the investors and the main economic agents over the rest of the economic "players" are also associated with it.

The weak economy is one of the preconditions of emergence of the expected currency crises. The longer is the stagnation the greater is the risk for the currency

† Index of the speculative attack, which is measured by the exchange rate as well as the volume of the international reserves and the interest rates.

crises. In such cases, main macroeconomic indicators reflect probability of the currency crises.

In total, the financial and currency crises emerge in effect of instable politics manifesting itself in the events which are easily seen through the empirically noticeable events: in existence of high interest rates and problems of the banking sector, in frequent political changes and employment rates etc. It is true that worsening of the macroeconomic situation is a precondition for the currency crisis yet it is insufficient for its real development.

In the economic literature maximum interval between the warning indicators of the crises and emergence of the crisis is considered to be 24 hours (in case of a balance of payment crisis) and 12 months for all other cases (for instance, worsening of the reserves for M3 indicator) (Tomczynka, M., 2000, p.17). Concretely, according to the priorities, we will distinguish only those 10 indicators which have been recognized in most of the economic literature (Kaminsky, G., Lizondo, S., Reinhart, C., 1998). These are as follows:

- From the point of view of the monetary policy: real exchange rate; international reserves; credit growth; inflation;
- From the point of view of fiscal policy: fiscal deficiency; crediting the government;
- According to the real sector: the GDP growth; employment/correlation of unemployment;
- According to the foreign sector: the trade balance.

Concrete changes of these indicators before and after the crisis are different from each other: before the crisis (approximately one year earlier), the indicators such as correlation with the M2/reserves and fiscal deficit as well as with interior credit/GDP keep growing. These indicators would decrease after the crisis but before the crisis, the indicators such as the GDP and the international reserves get also reduced; in addition, the export-import indicators keep worsening as well.

Despite the fact that the above mentioned indicators are universal, economic, financial and social conditions indicated by each of them acquire a very special meaning and their analysis create a precondition for prevention of emergence of the crises.

2.3. The Institutional Preconditions of the Currency Crisis

Peculiarities of emergence of the currency crisis are interconnected with the economic agents and the optimistic and pessimistic expectations for the behavior of the government.

When the artificially existing balance rate is not fixed and there are certain limits for free fluctuation, the government is responsible for maintaining stability within the amplitude of such fluctuations. When the disorders arise during the money supply process and the monetary mass increases in circulation, in the conditions of creeping currency regime the exchange rate gets reduced. In case the feeling of responsibility for the currency rate is strong enough on behalf of the government, then the market agents (the financial institutions) develop optimistic expectations and attach priority not to the increase of the monetary amounts but to its decrease and not to devaluation of the national currency, but to its growth. They sell out foreign currency and the exchange rate keeps growing.

Contrary to this is a pessimistic expectation which strengthens the pressure on the exchange rate. Periodical growth of the monetary mass undertaken by the government for the purpose of maintaining the value of the national currency within a definite range generates expectations among the economic agents for the decrease of national currency rate. The latter hasten the process by getting rid of the national currency and relevantly, the exchange rate gets reduced too.

When the public no more trusts the behavior of the government then the economic agents develops the feeling of uncertainty and their performance becomes unpredictable. The currency shock develops in the course of casual disorders; at such times the government tries to correct the situation (in ultimate cases it even changes the policies) and eventually, this action is followed by the growth of the monetary mass in circulation. The efforts of the government – to keep the currency within a particular range – become futile. The market agents perceive the devaluation of the exchange rate as a symptom of emergency of future fundamental problem and they try to purchase the foreign currency instead of selling it. Therefore, they will turn into the factors of destabilization. Because of such a destabilization effect, sometimes the government starts intervention at the inter-bank stock exchange earlier than usual which makes the credibility of the currency exchange rate even more suspicious, weakens the confidence of the market agents, and strengthens uncertainty at the market.

On the basis of all the statements above, we can conclude that the behavior of the government and the economic agents determines the changes of the exchange rate and creates institutional conditions for developing the currency crisis.

The government itself serves as a circumstance for enhancing the currency risks, which on the other hand, is trying to escape these risks through employing various tools. Three forms of government actions can be distinguished;

1. **Compensation.** During the period of the crisis the government is trying actively to compensate the losses. It is impossible to maintain the artificially balanced exchange rate if the government tries to compensate the lost reserves to be compatible with the expectations of the market agents. Putting emphasis over the money supply as a change to the lost reserves during the speculative attack, will create opportunities for the exchange rate, the prices and the interest rates to be kept stable but under one condition: if the money supply is changed in the form of capital flows whereas the decrease of the foreign reserves will be compensated by way of the growth of the internal credits. During the speculative attacks the reserves get exhausted, the freely floating exchange regime is established, the market balance grows dependant on the pace of growth of the internal debts and on the internal and foreign policy as well as on the interest rates. Internal credit becomes the main instrument for resolving the difficulties related to the free exchange rate. In fact, the emphasis on the currency markets will be shifted to the markets of financial liabilities because the aspiration of the government to compensate the reserves implies widening of the internal debt and thus, directing it towards purchasing the state liabilities;
2. **Administration.** It is connected with the expectation of the speculative pressure. The market participants are not sure when such a pressure will be undertaken and to what extent the exchange rate will be changed. Uncertainty of critical character is created. It will be even more strengthened by the government when it loudly makes prognosis on the expected speculative attacks as well as emergence of uncertainty and for the purpose of escaping it the government starts administrative pressure in order to maintain the balance.
3. **Prevention.** The government shifts its political efforts to all those remedies, which will help to avoid the crisis. Such remedies as for instance, attracting foreign loans, control over the capital etc. block the ways of spread of the crisis but are unable to prevent it. A vivid example of this is the Asian crisis of the 90s.

The pre-crisis situation in the countries is preconditioned by the irregular and controversial domestic policies in financing the budget deficit. It is based on emission of the securities and increase of internal debts. The private sector tries to take advantage of this situation and gain profits by speculative behavior. This type of policy can be continued until the central bank owns enough currency reserves. The economic agents, operating on the outer markets try to get ready by the moment when the central bank reserves will reach a critical point. Therefore, their attacks against the market become systematic and because of that, the currency market grows even more strained. On certain stages these attacks are successful and the "shadow floating currency rate" is formed as a result. The more the central bank becomes weak in stability of the currency rate, the stronger the free exchange rate grows and the speculative attacks against it stop operating.

When the international reserves of the central bank are large and the interior credits issued to the government are small in scale, then the artificially balanced currency exchange rate acquires safety for a long period of time and the speculative attacks prove unproductive, because only the agents provoking such attacks against the market lose their profits. Disintegration of the currency balance takes place after the international reserves are exhausted. In addition, the more the central bank issues interior credits to the government, the deeper the discrepancies will become; and finally, the higher the elasticity of the interest rates the quicker the currency crisis will set in. After exhaustion of the bank reserves, speculative attacks against the exchange rate prove to be more effective.

The basis for such a scenario is formed by the peculiarities of the speculative pressures over the currency market. It was based upon the simple and credible mechanical policy practiced by the government. The government is eligible to reduce the problems of the balance of payment which makes the fiscal policy more acute and the central bank, apart from interventions against the exchange rate and making the monetary policies stricter, possesses other instruments as well; yet use of these instruments is connected with compromising between the short-term and long-term economic goals.

The countries tend to be alike with regard to the behavior of their governments during the speculative pressure (when they are restricted in free actions) and this happens because of the political and economic obstacles. In such cases, speculative attacks of the market agents against the currency create objective economic conditions for devaluation. The government, on the other hand, owns limited currency resources in order to protect the currency exchange rate. In its turn, the reserves determine the profits that the market dealers should get.

When the government reserves are far more than the reserves that the market dealers own, then the resources sold to the government by the market dealers prove to be enough for the government to maintain the currency balance, but meanwhile, resources of the economic agents get subsided. This process is called the "high reserve game". In a contrary case which is called the "low reserve game", the government reserves are so scanty that any player (or an economic agent) is eligible to establish an artificial exchange rate. If a single agent sells out all his/her national currency then he/she will get profits but if all of the agents decide to sell the resources at one time, then they will get only a part from their profits from the government reserves.

There is another game as well, when not a single agent is eligible to get profits independently from the government. This may only happen if all the agents sell their resources at one time (simultaneously). At such moments, structure of the profits of the economic agents acquires the following form: single dealers start an attack and suffer the losses. They will be unable to maintain profits without selling the national currency that they posses. When all the economic agents undertake an attack, then each of them have a chance to profit; when all of them are in attack, then the exchange rate gets low, but if all the economic agents are hardly sure of their success and therefore, only a part of them engage themselves in the attack, then maintaining the balanced exchange rate becomes a reality. During the joint attack of the economic agents the government takes the function of a mediator, which implies utilization of the governmental reserves as well. This will enhance emergence of a shaky currency exchange rate.

The economic agents always make attempts to violate the balance whereas the efforts of the government are directed at neutralizing them. Such activities were not so intensive as to neutralize attacks of the dealers, but they were not so weak as to allow the inevitable change of the course either. Economic agents can always join their forces in order to violate the balance.

In general, financial discrepancies start because the government tries to escape the upcoming crisis detoriariations and for this purpose it undertakes some expenditure.

When expectancy emerges in the market that the free floating exchange rate is going to be established because of gradual devaluation of the national currency, the government will find it more and more difficult to restore the previous balance since the changes of the currency rate become dependant on the personal perception of the agents. In such conditions, even the least activity undertaken by the economic agents would violate the balance.

There are many enhancing conditions which may violate the currency balance. The profits increase in case the issuance of the monetary banknotes goes down which is the main symptom indicating that the economic agents should start pressure over the currency market. The currency structure of the state debt may worsen the crisis even more. Increase of the interest rates which follows devaluation of the national currency poses an option before the government: either bankruptcy of the banks or a quickly devaluated currency. Increase of the interest rates causes redistribution of the profits which may not at all be desirable for the government.‡

During the recent years, along with strengthening the national currency, increase of the prices on the interest rates and real estate was also notable; meanwhile, the bank deposits were also rising. In Great Britaindeveloped market countries the financial savings were distributed through the alternative and competitive spheres whereas in the post-Soviet countries distribution of the financial savings took place not on the basis of competition among the real estate markets and the commercial banks, but according to what extent would the national currency maintain its value which in its turn implies expectancy of hidden devaluation of the national currency.

Peculiarity of this scenario is that violation of the balance of the exchange rate, in order to protect strict parity of the exchange procedure is based on the extra expenditure undertaken by the government, whereas the economic agents do not comply with the state policy and are looking forward to its collapse. Initially, this kind of a pessimistic expectancy emerges on the basis of the prognosis about worsening the economic situation of the country or based on a long-term depression of the economy.§ As a result of this, the speculative attacks start which makes the economic situation even worse and disruption of the economic balance undergoes through the self-realization regime. The economic agents assume that if they don't sell the national currency they will lose the profits and will be unable to protect their income because the old exchange rate would be cancelled. Expectancy of the self-realization of the crisis is based upon the joint actions of the market agents which are projected to getting short-term profits. Their manipulations strengthen disruption of the balance.

Change of the currency exchange rate can also be caused by a strained political situation, which makes the population feel pessimistic because of the expected riot. At the background of such tendencies, the agents start exercising pressure upon the currency market and as a consequence of this, the banking system collapses giving way to the currency crisis.

‡ For instance, in Great Britain, in 1992, increase of the prices on real estate lowered the amount of deposits in the commercial banks. A contrary event took place in Georgia, Russia, Armenia and other countries

§ For instance, such a symptom may be worsening of the labor market conditions.

In all countries, the currency crises develop under various scenarios and the "infection" becomes contagious in different ways. Nevertheless, everywhere, the stimulator of the crises was a speculative attack against the national currency. Reaction of the government on the speculative attack against the national currency represents a reflection of the economic situation existing in the country. Accordingly, along with the global order, the crises reveal the economic peculiarities of the country.

2.4. Peculiarities of the Crisis in the Post-Soviet Countries

In the 90s, all along the post-Soviet countries, profundity and duration of the fall of the GDP level considerably surpassed similar events going on in Central and Eastern Europe (see Figure 2).

Financial crises embraced the post-Soviet countries quite easily. In this, the main role was played by the Russian crisis, which spread across other countries as well because of the tight trade, financial and economic links which were still maintained by inertia.

Why were the banking and currency crises so profound?

Under the interpretation of the supporters of the neoclassical trend, the currency crises that took place in Russia and other post-communist countries emerged due to the wrong policies. The state regulated banking system also contributed to the development of the crisis. According to the idea of the institutionalists, the banking crisis was originated because the role of the banks as of the mediators was very weak; the same way feeble was the financial regulation and the burden of risky credits was too heavy. The Russian crisis on the other hand, was accompanied by the criminalization of economy, which had been pending from the previous times. On the whole, the financial crisis was preconditioned by wrong regulation of the financial instruments and abundant emission of the securities.

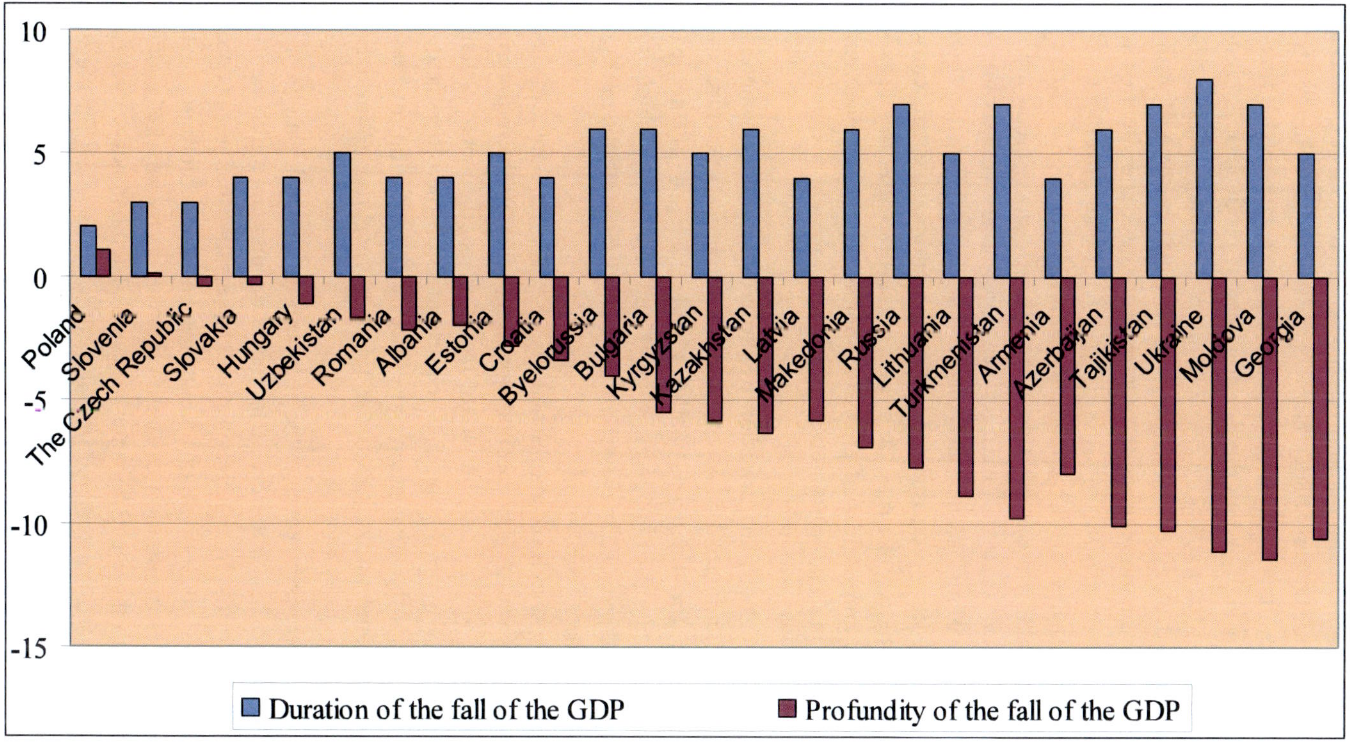

The source: World Bank (1998). p. 6.

Figure 2. Duration and profundity of the fall of the GDP in the post-communist countries in 90,s

Banks are real creators of the market. Being the "mediators" they establish contacts between the producers and the consumers as well as between the owners of the money and the money-lenders. Enterprising is based upon the financial support of the banks, especially when the development of production is hindered by insufficient savings at the market. In the conditions of scanty savings a lot of commercial banks issued credits by the loans taken from the central bank. In addition, absence of coordination among the enterprises caused the situation when the debts were not paid. In effect, emission grew even higher (we mean liberal policies which developed in a distorted form and took the form of transfers and which was nicknamed "the atmospheric transfer"). Growth of the credit amounts and the credit expansion was followed by wasting money, non-commodity operations and increase of inflation. Later on, it was changed by the contrary radical measures: the credits were restricted and on the initial stage, this caused a catastrophic growth of the interest rates. Just like in the first case, this proved to be the most unattractive and useless of all the economic regulation mechanisms. Reorganization of the financial system was also developing in a non-effective way.

In this period, the goal of transformation was to create a relevant context for the economic growth. It required: 1. Existence of the relatively stable currency; 2. Accurate fulfillment of the financial liabilities and existence of the market mediators; 3. Implementation of moderate budget and tax policy which would enhance expansion of the production. These are the factors defining the profundity of the crises in the countries.

According to the research accomplished by the World Bank, the crisis situation of the countries was mostly preconditioned by ignoring the requirements of the market discipline, which is an important factor of macroeconomic stability and the economic growth. Ignoring the said requirements on the other hand, is a prerequisite for creating influential groups in effect of privatization, increase of the tax debts and irrational utilization of the financial resources (World Bank, 2002.).

A dispute is undergoing among the economists on relevancy of the recognized amount of losses with regard to recession and unemployment rate during the economic reforms. In practice, such a conversation has not been clear cut in relation with the post-communist countries because according to their characteristic features, transformation of these countries to the market economy was unique with regard to those accompanying events which had never ever taken place neither in nature nor in history before. Accordingly, the quest for the ways of escaping economic and financial crises continued through experiments and errors committed in the meantime. Although, it is anyway obvious that the transactional expenditures of the transition period were manifested in high hyperinflation and decrease of the pace of economic growth, which in its turn, was caused by underdevelopment of the market institutions and weakly regulated financial structures.

The Financial Crisis in Russia

In August of 1998, Russia was obsessed with the crisis, in which the currency and banking crises were intermingled; the reason for emergence of such a crisis was the financial policy wrongly practiced by the state.

In 1995–1997, Russia's state budget was extremely deficient. In order to cover the deficit the Russian government periodically increased its financial liabilities by way of issuing the state securities to be realized at the domestic as well as the world markets. These actions were targeted at enhancing the might of the national currency and attracting the loans. Hyper-obsession with such policy bore a negative effect. The cost of the released securities exceeded the 15% of the GDP in 1997. Servicing the state debts and covering a part of it commanded another emission, yet increase of emissions enhanced building of a "financial pyramid" and meant increase of the interest rates on the state securities which eventually would lead to inevitable crisis.

Emission of the securities as the source of filling the budget gradually started to resemble a dangerous game. The ministry of finance increased the expenditures in order to cover the debts. The generated income and the balance of expenditures for servicing it grew less and less profitable for the budget. Yet a year earlier, emission of the securities kept losing its significance.

Adequate reaction to the state policy was initiated by the domestic as well as the foreign economic agents. In effect of this, the amount of foreign investments and realization of the securities decreased; the Russian balance of payment was worsened; demand on the securities was sharply reduced. On top of all this, in the third quarter of 1998 the time set in, when the greater part of the securities had to be reimbursed. This period was also accompanied by the crisis when devaluation of the Russian ruble turned inevitable.

Decrease of demand at the Russian securities market was mostly preconditioned by the mistrust of the foreign investors with regard to the liabilities taken by the Russian state. Increase of the budget deficit seemed clear. This situation was aggravated by the decrease of the prices on the main export product — oil and gas — throughout the world markets, which reduced the income of the budget; meanwhile, in order to stabilize the exchange rate of the ruble the Central Bank was spending the golden fund supplies. Foreign investors extended due efforts to save their capital from the expected devaluation of ruble by getting rid of the Russian currency and this situation became instrumental in hastening the process on the whole.

In 1997-1998, the amount of oil and the oil products increased on the world markets and the prices were reduced to almost 40%. The world prices fell on other raw materials as well. In effect of this, the oil exports from Russia were reduced two times. In order to avoid the oil crisis, the oil producing countries agreed on the decrease of production of the said products, yet this remedy turned to be too late for Russia. According to the data provided by the IMF, as a result of decrease of the prices on the oil products worldwide, the losses that Russia suffered only from the oil-products amounted to 2.8 billion dollars. One of the ways of compensating this loss was to apply for a loan to the international financial organizations.

In addition, in order to cover the debt of securities to the foreign creditors, Russia was obliged to issue the Euro-bonds which would diminish the reserve currency fund of that country. On top of it, by purchasing the Euro-bonds, Russia was no more able to fill in the budget because the annual interest for serving the debt exceeded 30%.

In order to escape the crisis Russian government undertook the following actions:

1. In order to neutralize devaluation of the ruble and for the purpose of reducing the demand on the currency means, the Russian government introduced additional customs duty amounting to 3% and by this action restricted imports;
2. In the beginning, in order to maintain the exchange rate of the ruble the Central Bank increased the currency amounts. In effect of this, the currency and gold reserves were considerably decreased (by 17 billion dollars), which constituted approximately 8$ of the Central Bank reserves;
3. The Central Bank established strict rules on purchasing the currency. Initially, this situation required transfer of the ruble instead of the currency which drove many banks into insolvency. In addition, demands on the currency sharply decreased and the currency corridor was increased up to 2-3 times. It was followed by a contrary reaction of the market: the currency rose up in price, the costs for the imported commodities also jumped up and the operations were frozen on the securities' market.

4. In the middle of August, commercial banks were temporarily forbidden to repay the debts on credits taken from the foreign banks.

Thus, as a result of the crisis of financial policy, the state lost the confidence of the investors. The Central Bank was obliged to close the currency market and the state partially denied its obligations. Overall, in 1998 the official exchange rate of the US dollar to the Russian rouble rose from 5.96 to 20.65 rubles to the dollar, or 3.46 times.

In effect of weakening of the national currency, in fact, "dollarization" of Russia's economy took place. Administrative measures taken by the Russian government proved insufficient for escaping the economic crisis. Those measures only envisaged administrative interference and in fact, equaled to suspension of the economic reforms.

The Russian financial crisis rippled (under the "Domino principle") across the countries which were still maintaining tight economic links with Russia. The crisis in Ukraine, along with some other factors, was caused by the low pace of imported capital, accumulation of foreign as well as domestic debts and other interior problems pending in the country. Abrupt fall of the economy was characteristic to Byelorussia as well and therefore, the financial collapse was not at all unexpected for a country which anyway was plunged in a crisis. It's true that the Baltic countries managed to protect their currency from devaluation, but according to the calculations made by the experts, they still experienced certain losses.

The Financial Crisis Dissemination in Post-Communist Countries

The crisis of 1998 in Russia made a ripple reaction (an indirect "Domino effect") on the economy of other post-Soviet countries and on former Socialist countries, too. In these countries, as a result of the crisis, the currency rate fell down considerably, the prices increased and the development pace decreased as well.

The influence of the "financial shock" from Russia was preconditioned by insufficiency of the economic reforms in post-communist countries and the pessimistic expectancy of the economic agents there. Devaluation of the national currency bore a new wave of inflation, caused decrease of demand on the national currency and brought about the stagnation of the GDP growth.

Aspirations of the government to control inflation was a natural development. Liberalization of the prices enhanced distribution of the resources and increase of the prices and in parallel to this, this process was expedited by expectations for the price rise. Liberalization of foreign trade increased the monetary mass in foreign currency even more. Increase of money supply provoked an increase in prices, during the course of which inflation turned into hyperinflation. It was followed by the increase of the interest rates on the financial assets which accelerated capitalization of the savings in the financial sector. Thus, speculative increase in prices of assets in the financial sector brought about a decrease of investments and production in the real sector. This was a general scenario of development of the post-Soviet countries, which later on turned into a more acute process by initiation of the global financial-currency crises

The results of financial crisis showed up in the real sector as well as on the political arena. The national currency turned out to be devaluated to a larger extent which proved enough to disrupt the economy which had been shaky before.

Devaluation of the national currency rate was enhanced by the overwhelming aspiration of the Central Banks to maintain the exchange rate of the national currency. The behavior of the governments resembled the events that are depicted in a classical scenario, in which the economic agents (in order to protect their income) applied to a tested trick and by way of extending pressure over the currency market, aggravated the crisis even more. By this, the currency market became restricted, and thus, demand on the foreign currency increased. Restriction of the market, expectation of the agents and psychological fear made mistrust of national currency more profound, and its rate fell even lower. The administrative rule of supervision over the exchange regime restricted the regulatory function of the market and therefore, it failed to make an expected positive effect on the stabilization of the currency rate.

The above-mentioned events were preceded by a decrease of the budget gains, arrears in delivering salaries and pensions, increase of the state debt and reduction of imports.

The central banks yielded to overall agitation and opposed the psychological pressure (which had already been started) connected with conversion of national curencies with restricting the currency exchange, broadening the currency interventions at the inter-bank stock exchange and wasted reserves on the useless policy of strengthening the national currency exchange rate. As the agitation grew higher, the central Bank reserves kept decreasing. The commercial banks proved unable to launch large-scale exchange operations and failed to satisfy the demand on the foreign currency, too. They had to face the danger of the crisis, because the amounts at their disposal grew lower and restriction of the market, decrease of the number of the agents and the psychological pressure made the fall of the national currency exchange rate even more intensive.

Along the expected complications in the banking system, the exchange rates grow even higher and thus financial panic is initiated. In the post-Soviet countries of 1997–98, the financial crisis was preceded by an increase in differences among interest rates, deposits and loans which turned out to be the signal for the expected disruption of the financial balance (see Figure 3).

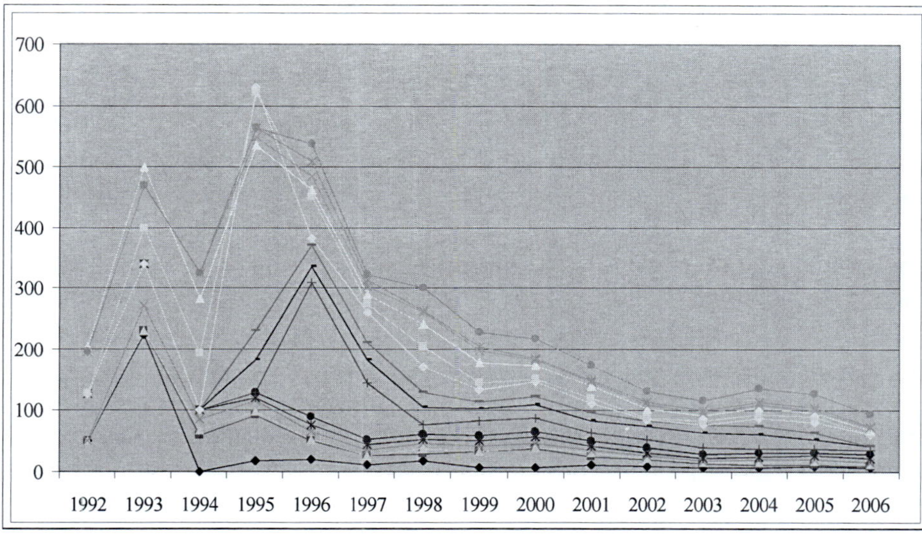

The source: EBRD

Figure 3. Coefficient of the interest rates (correlation of the interest rates to the deposits with the interest rates on the loans).

The answers turned out to be controversial to the question: what was more important in violation of the currency balance – worsening of the banking system and economic situation or the financial-currency panic?

Disruption of balance is related to the microeconomic problems of the financial institutions which bring about the speculative attack against the currency regime. In particular, as a result of issuing morally risky credits undertaken by the non-regulated banks and the financial institutions, non-liquid credits and abundant capital investments enter the economic field. The collapse becomes inevitable when the government tries to introduce guarantees on the assets. The subsidies reveal the deficit of the government budget whereas the bank credits disclose the government debts. The market agents are prepared and in waiting before the moment when the financial crisis starts and the government will take relevant steps to save the financial institutions. Disruption of the currency balance is a result of the market reaction to such behavior of the government. This is the outcome of the miscarriages of implementation of structural regulations and fiscal expenditure of the financial restructuring as well as manifestation of the expected reduction of the fiscal deficit and downfall of economic activities. Because of weak supervision over the expansionist financial mediation, non-liquid loans emerge and abundant investments and artificially puffed up assets are also created. In such conditions, any opportunity of leading a well structured macroeconomic policy is just an illusion.

Panicking of the international investors, mistakes of the local government and weak programs of the international aid organizations, along with bankruptcy of the banks and political destabilization will eventually cause "ousting" of foreign capital from the markets (which later on will turn into currency crisis).

According to the ideas of certain authors, the basis for such a crisis can be the abundant capital investment in the enterprises, which will precondition deficit of the current account (Blaszkewicz, M., 2000, p. 20). Reduction of the private capital flow as well as sharp fall of the bank and non-bank loans will be followed by increase of demand on them.

This is also connected with the miscarriages in bank management. In particular, in order to compensate the losses inflicted by management, by way of exercising preliminary pressure over the markets, the mediator banks will try to make the investments liquid, but as a result of decrease of foreign investments and credits they will be deprived of the capacity of liquidation and they will lose the capital as well. Panic will spread across the banks and eventually, it will give rise to economic and political disorders.

The currency relations among the countries have many aspects which reflect only in a unified form whatever has happened in reality and whatever may happen in future. It can't be discarded either that disruption of the exchange rate will start with only a few problems but later on, will be transformed into radical changes. It became clear that the financial crises start with worsening of he economic situation which is followed by the economic pressure undertaken for the purpose of gaining a short-term success. Self-realization of the crisis starts in effect of speculative attacks of the economic agents. In such conditions, variations of the exchange rate reveal the complex situation in economy and in such circumstances, actions undertaken by the foreign investors will turn into an accelerator of the currency crises. In case there's no expectancy of worsening of the economic situation, the reaction of local and foreign investors turns to be self-contradictory. The first ones try to purchase the foreign currency and the latter aspire to save the investments. The above-mentioned reactions which initially have individual character and are based on individual information, afterwards acquire collective character and by way of imitating each other, the pre-crisis panic spreads in a "ripple reaction". The financial balance becomes disrupted and a contagious infection of the currency crisis emerges which later on spreads across the countries linked among each other by trade relations. Speculative attacks of the economic agents are successful in the countries where the export production is generated, but in the countries where such production is sold as a substitute to the local product, the government (in order to protect the local production from competitive conditions) "is forced" to undertake devaluation of the national currency. Most frequently, main reasons of generation of financial crises are the errors committed in the banking sector to which the economic agents make an instantaneous reaction

On the whole, in the 90's characteristic feature of the post-Soviet countries was discretional financial-currency policy seasoned with certain elements of monetary and inflation targeting. Fear of free floating regime of the currency was also characteristic to them. After the crisis of 1998, this fear was neutralized, although, it turned that the quasi-fixed regime of the exchange rate would be unable to ensure gradual reduction of inflation.

Fiscal deficit and high-rate inflation is a characteristic feature for the post-Soviet countries. To some extent, it becomes a precondition of panic and the group pressure of the economic agents upon the financial markets (Stiglitz J., 1998. Radelet S.& Sachs J.,1998).

Increase of mistrust of the economic agents towards the national currency was the precondition of development of all the above said events. As a result, GDP growth after the crisis in 1999 remained much lower in comparison to 1989 (see table 5).

Table 5. Real GDP in 1999 compared to 1989 (1989=100)

Azerbaijan	46
Byelorussia	75
Estonia	76
Latvia	60
Lithuania	65
Moldova	30
Russia	53

Table 5. (Continued)

Georgia	33
Armenia	42
Tajikistan	43
Turkmenistan	53
Ukraine	35
Uzbekistan	89
Kazakhstan	59
Kyrgyzstan	62
Average pot-communist countries	53
Easter Europea and Baltic Countries and CIS	77
Poland	121
Albania	91
Bolgaria	66
croatia	79
Chech Republic	95
Hungary	99
Romania	74
Slovakia	101
Slovenia	107
Easter Europea and Baltic Countries	101

Source: EBRD

Chapter 3

Foreign Exchange Policy in the Post-Soviet Countries

3.1. Evolution and Controversies of the Foreign Exchange Policy

At the end of the 1990s, the countries in transition accomplished the institutional changes and by way of employing various financial policies achieved the level of inflation amounting to less than 10%. In the same period, a number of risks were revealed which then created the preconditions for the spread of the currency crisis and, afterwards, compelled the countries to revise their monetary policy. It turned out that the countries with the fixed exchange rate (for instance, the Baltic countries) were restricted in implementing the anti-inflation policy. On the other hand, for maintaining the enthusiasm of foreign investors, regulation of the national currency would be rather unattractive and it would also create danger of inflation. According to different conditions in the development of the countries, four systems of monetary regulation were formed:

1. The countries (the Baltic countries and Bulgaria), which made it their goal to maintain the fixed currency exchange rate and targeted inflation, established regimes similar to the Currency Boards;*
2. Another group of the countries (Kazakhstan, Georgia and Armenia) directed their efforts to targeting inflation.

* Although, the Currency Boards in a classical form are still non-operational in those countries.

3. The third group of countries (Russia, for instance) targeted implementation of the anti-inflation policy.
4. The countries attributed to the fourth group are an overwhelming majority of the post-Soviet countries (Azerbaijan, Moldova, Turkmenistan, Tajikistan, Ukraine, Uzbekistan), which are engaged in implementation of the so-called "mixed policies" and along with keeping inflation low, they are projected toward optimization of the exchange rate as well.

Initially, the countries with the fixed exchange rate were characterized by a high level of hyperinflation. The central banks were attributed only a restricted role in crediting the commercial banks, whereas they were financing the governments in a broader way. Foreign banks and the companies had a large share in the financial markets. This and many other factors prompted the Baltic countries in the beginning of the 90s to link their own national currency to the currency of those foreign countries, which were distinguished by relative stability and at the same time, were donors to them. The German Mark became such a currency to the Baltic countries; nevertheless, the said countries still needed 6 years on average to reach an inflation level amounting to 10%.

Stability of the national currency is a criterion of the effectiveness of the monetary policy of the above-mentioned countries, although it should be noted that at the expense of this, they rejected use of the monetary policy and created liberal currency legislation. Such countries are small in size and, therefore, they are less attractive for serious financial monopolies that would undertake import of the speculative capital in their markets. Accordingly, their balance of payment is less shaky. In addition, in the above-mentioned countries, the central banks maintained the function of supervision over the commercial banks, yet they proved unable to escape the financial crises of 1995-96.

We wouldn't assert that such a policy is the only way for achieving stability or vice versa. The fact is that the national bank, besides forming the regime of the currency council, possesses other instruments, too, for maintaining the stability of the national currency.

The countries oriented toward targeting inflation, before they reached a low level of inflation, introduced the so-called corridors for reducing inflation. Such a corridor was also set for the interest rates as well (Hungary). Some countries made a shift from the fixed currency regime to the targeted inflation (Armenia) and put emphasis on the pure inflation indicator.[†] In other countries, the profit rates and

† This indicator excludes the prices, tariffs and indirect taxes established by the state.

the operations with the securities undertaken in open markets were used as the tools for influencing inflation (Georgia, Poland). In addition to this, the budget policies implemented by the national bank and the government turned out to be openly controversial. The policy of targeted inflation proved successful in those countries where these discrepancies were institutionally regulated and agreement was reached in order to undertake the budget expenditures in a goal-oriented manner with the inflation rate taken in view. In other countries, where the institutional regulation was not ensured and the central bank as well as the government was implementing the policy of neutralizing each other, the economy was developing gradually, step by step. Along with reduction of inflation the pace of economic growth and the budget profits also decreased. Such a situation is based on the policy of the floating exchange rates of the currency. The question of an alternative between devaluation of the currency and inflation became prominent, although, unlike other countries, in Kazakhstan, decrease of the exchange rate of the currency and inflation took place simultaneously.

Most of the post-Soviet countries employed the mixed policies. The monetary policy was concentrated on regulation of the exchange rate. Characteristic features of the transitional countries was a prevailing share of the foreign currency in the national economy and weak participation of the local financial and banking systems in the economic activities. Accordingly, the manageable floating currency regime became a characteristic feature to many former Soviet countries and a number of European states as well. Participation of foreign capital in the post-Soviet countries endangered the operation of those commercial banks which did not own diversified credits and the foreign currency occupied a considerable part in their portfolios. In the non-liquidity conditions the mentioned banks found themselves under some risks. In order to save them, the central bank issued short-term credits, but in other countries, participation of the foreign currency in the bank portfolios rescued them from the crises (Georgia).

Despite the fact that stability of the national currency endogenically represents support as well as opposition of the economic agents to the policy being carried out by the government, in the post-Soviet countries, exogenically, there are several reasons for deterioration of the currency and financial balance, which run as follows:

- Fundamental problems characteristic to the typically underdeveloped economy in the post-Soviet countries:‡ the budget deficit, state debt, low

‡ In the oil producing countries, such as Russia, Kazakhstan, Azerbaijan and Turkmenistan the "Dutch illness" enhances the growth of public revenues but the budget is yet deficient.

monetization of the country's economy, weak banking system and insufficient progress in terms of institutional and structural reforms;

Table 6. The share of broad money (M2) in the GDP

	1992	1993	1994	1995	1996	1997	1998	1999	2000	2001	2002	2003	2004	2005	2006
Azerbaijan	38.6	54.8	55.9	9.0	8.8	9.9	7.1	7.4	6.9	6.6	6.7	7.3	8.0	6.3	12.0
Byelorussia		20.9	39.0	14.8	14.2	15.8	30.9	16.4	17.2	15.2	15.0	16.8	17.7	19.3	22.1
Estonia		28.3	27.0	25.1	26.6	29.8	27.3	32.2	34.5	37.7	37.3	37.8	39.7	47.7	51.8
Latvia		28.5	30.1	20.3	20.1	24.0	23.2	23.4	26.9	29.5	32.4	35.3	38.6	43.1	48.4
Lithuania	39.2	23.1	25.8	22.0	16.8	18.5	18.8	20.7	22.8	26.1	28.6	30.9	34.9	40.7	43.7
Moldova	43.5	19.1	14.3	17.1	16.6	19.5	14.9	14.7	15.7	18.2	20.0	20.4	25.4	29.5	28.3
Russia			19.0	16.0	15.5	14.4	16.0	17.0	14.6	15.8	18.0	19.7	24.3	26.0	27.9
Georgia			5.6	5.0	6.7	8.0	6.4	7.9	10.3	11.1	11.6	12.4	15.2	16.4	19.3
Armenia					8.2	8.7	10.0	11.0	14.7	13.4	15.6	14.4	15.0	16.3	18.2
Tajikistan				19.1	8.3	8.6	7.1	6.7	8.2	7.9	8.4	8.3	7.0	7.6	9.4
Turkmenistan		18.9	25.6	18.8	8.1	10.2	15.0	12.7	19.4	16.1	13.0	13.9	12.9	13.0	12.7
Ukraine	0.0	50.0	32.5	26.7	12.6	11.1	13.3	15.0	16.6	18.5	22.1	28.5	35.3	36.4	43.8
Uzbekistan	52.0	53.3	34.7	18.2	21.0	17.5	15.4	13.6	12.2	12.4	10.6	10.3	12.2	14.4	15.1
Kazakhstan			27.9	13.1	11.4	9.9	10.3	8.6	13.6	15.3	17.1	19.2	21.1	27.8	27.2
Kyrgyzstan				17.2	13.6	13.7	14.5	13.6	11.3	11.1	14.6	17.5	20.6	21.2	28.6

The source: EBRD

- Low pace of transformation and weak performance of the market mechanisms. Strong administrative interference in the work of the marker institutions was a hindering factor to the development of the private sector and stimulated corruption as well as establishing anew public oligarchy. After privatization of the enterprises, control over them was undertaken by the oligarchic circles, who instead of creating a competitive environment were more interested in creating the "green house" conditions for their capital. Real economy was developing very slowly.[§] In addition to that, mistrust to the government created a

§ Except for the oil-producing countries.

psychological expectation among the people with regard to repetition of deterioration of the economic balance.

- Low level of monetization, at the background of the limited role of the banks. Development of the banks under conditions of a low amount of deposited savings, high rate of cash clearings and better trust in the foreign currency is going on in a restricted area.
- The low level of monetization is an indicator of less stability (because the nominal changes of the money do not change even in a minimal way its correlation, and the exchange rate as well as the prices react in a painful way to the changes of money).Yet the slightest growth of the monetary mass will have a very significant impact on the exchange rate;
- Weakness of the banks and a high share of shadow economy in industrial production commands no trust and the opportunities of increase of demand on the national currency tend to be relevantly restricted;
- Indicators of instability of the economy: low level of investment flow, weak banking system and a scanty amount of savings. Stagnation of the economy, on the other hand, provokes frustration and a feeling of hopelessness among the people;
- Deficit of trust and confidence in economy; lack of the long-term bank credits is an indicator of this;
- Lack of international reserves;
- Small role of the banking-financial mediator. The coefficient of monetization is a telling example of this. Compared to the countries of central and eastern Europe, it is twice less than in the post-Soviet countries (see Figure3).
- One of the hindering factors in the development of the banking system is the foreign currency used in commercial banking activities. In such economies, the role of the exchange rate is of paramount importance. It determines the level of prices by means of the imported and exported prices and strengthens the dependence of the country on the outer world; **
- Lack of the amount of deposits in the banks with regard to the GDP. Despite the fact that the credit supply allocated to the economy by the banks is growing on a regular basis, its indicator to the GDP amounts to

** In some experts' opinion, the countries which have a higher share of foreign trade in their GDP and a low level of monetization, should aspire either to the analogy of the currency board practiced in the Baltic countries or to introducing foreign currency (Dollar or Euro) as the only means of payment, which will assist these countries to escape the financial crisis. (Dombrovski M., 1999. p. 24).

20–30%, whereas in the central European countries this indicator is at least twice as much. In addition to this, the amount of credits in the private sector is 15% on average and in the countries of central Europe and the Baltic countries this indicator is almost 2.5 times higher. ††

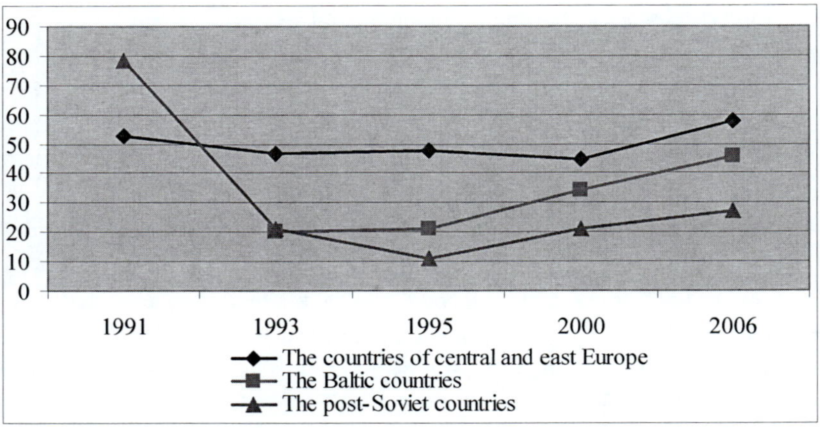

The source: World Development Indicators; Jarocinski M. (1998).

Figure 4. Monetization in the post-communist countries

This and other indicators as well do express the weak financial standing of the countries, but viewed in dynamics, during the last 5 years, at least slightly, they tend to improve their situation. The above-mentioned indicators are not sufficient to make us consider the endogenic origin of the deterioration of the financial-currency balance. Apart from the financial indicators, the behavior of the economic agents is determined by the macro-economic development of the country, its institutional regulations and by one most important factor: the political environment.

It should also be noted at this point, that in the post-communist countries, there still exist the circumstances which are hindering the deterioration of the financial balance. In particular, the financial markets are rather underdeveloped and therefore, the global currency crises hardly represent any serious danger to them at all. Besides, subsidizing the economy by the banks is restricted, the inter-bank competition is rather low and the credit deficit is outstanding; on the other hand, the low level of bank deposits is preconditioned by the fact that agriculture

†† World Development Indicators.

is holding a larger segment in the economy of the countries, where no banking operations are performed.

In addition, it should also be noted that the attitude and trust of the economic agents to the national currency and to the financial system in general, change together with the changes in politics. In order to achieve economic growth, it is not only enough that the government conceives the wish of combating poverty and corruption that had existed before. Economic stabilization depends on the duration of the expectancy of inflation and also on the trust which the government is granted for the purpose of settling numerous economic and social problems, for overcoming the factor of ambiguity and reducing the risk factors related to the investment activities.

3.2. Inflation or Exchange Rate?

In general, the exchange rate is never permanent; it changes along with current economic developments: according to the changes in prices on the goods and services on one hand and the changes in trade and foreign relations among the countries on the other.

Changes in the prices on the goods and services are an important factor in the variations of the exchange rates.

High-rate inflation is a characteristic feature for the post-Soviet countries. To some extent, it becomes a precondition of panic and the group pressure of the economic agents upon the financial markets (Stiglitz, 1998. Radelet and Sachs, 1998).

Inflation in post-communist countries at present is moderately high. To put it in simpler terms, increase in the prices is caused by the growth of the money in circulation. Hence, the government of the countries is facing a dilemma: either it should provide conversion of foreign currency into the national currency which implies increase of the money in circulation, or it should decrease the delivery of the national currency. Yet one type of measure excludes another. Delivery of national currency keeps inflation growing but removing it from circulation makes the national currency exchange rate even more stable.

Of course, such a situation will not last long. The monetary management would be granted the opportunity to revert to policies which will liberate it from the interventions at the inter-bank stock exchange; the exchange rate will also be formed without the involvement of the official management bodies. Thus, countries are facing an objective necessity of changing their monetary policies.

All the statements above represent an optimistic variant which is characteristic to countries which have escaped the stagnation period and are now facing an option in financial-currency policies.

Budget expenditure of the government is an important factor for maintaining balance in the financial-currency policy. The budget has an essential influence on formation of the currency rate to the extent that exceeding its expenditure will enhance increase of the income prices, because it implies the type of money in circulation which is obtained from taxes and has not been "earned" by way of economic production. The deficit expenditures, according to their nature equal to the "Dutch illness". It is typical especially to oil and gas producer countries (Azerbaijan, Turkmenista, Kasakhstan, Russia). If the budget rationalization is carried out within the decrease of inflation and, instead of deficit, surplus is planned, then the "Dutch illness" will be lessened, which later on, will have a positive influence on the stabilization of the countries.

In such conditions, the use of the monetary instruments by the Central Bank (even in the most unimportant ways) will create opportunities for keeping the inflation rate low.

In general, inflation is the phenomenon which reflects in a condensed way all the events going on in an economy, and you can only define it by way of explaining all the processes characteristic to macro-economics.

It is true that a relatively large mass of money is considered to be the reason for price growth but if inflation is really prone to the influence of the monetary factors for a long time-period, then in a short period of time the foreign investments, wages, the interest rates and prices will make an impact on it.

The conditions of initiating inflation are created. It is even more strained because of the foreign factors: by the price growth of energy resources, devaluation of the dollar and by increase of inflation in the countries which are the main trade partners and the so-called "Inflation import" are developed.

Neutralization of the enhancing factors of inflation growth is undertaken by means of the monetary mass and this, in fact, is carried out by using all the instruments at the disposal of the central Banks, which are: state securities, deposit certificates, reserve requirements, credits and deposit mechanisms, etc. Another important circumstance should also be noted here: changes of the monetary mass influence the exchange rate and, therefore, during regulation of the inflation and carrying out bilateral currency interventions, an alternative is created: either to maintain the existing currency rate or to allow inflation. Inflation also proves to have two sides: first, a necessary attribute to the economic activity and second, a hindering factor to it.

Table 7. Inflation in post-communist countries

	1996	1997	1998	1999	2000	2001	2002	2003	2004	2005	2006	2007	2008 Prel.
Post Soviet Countries													
Russia	47.8	14.7	27.6	86.1	20.8	21.6	15.7	13.7	10.9	12.7	9.7	9.0	11.5
Armenia	18.7	14.0	8.7	0.7	-0.8	3.1	1.1	4.7	7.0	0.6	2.9	4.3	5.7
Azerbaijan	19.7	3.5	-0.8	-8.5	1.8	1.5	2.8	2.2	6.7	9.6	8.3	16.7	19.5
Belarus	52.7	63.9	72.9	293.7	168.6	61.1	42.5	28.4	18.1	10.3	7.0	8.4	13.3
Georgia	39.4	7.1	3.6	19.2	4.1	4.6	5.7	4.9	5.7	8.4	9.2	9.3	9.0
Moldova	23.5	11.8	7.7	39.3	31.1	9.6	5.2	11.6	12.5	12.0	12.8	12.3	14.8
Ukraine	80.0	15.9	10.6	22.7	28.2	12.0	0.8	5.2	9.0	13.5	9.1	12.8	25.5
Kazakhstan	39.1	17.4	7.1	8.3	13.2	8.4	5.9	6.4	6.9	7.6	8.6	10.8	16.6
Kyrgyzstan	31.9	23.4	10.5	35.9	18.7	6.9	2.0	3.1	4.1	4.3	5.6	10.2	19.0
Tajikistan	418.5	88.0	43.2	27.5	32.9	38.6	12.2	16.4	7.2	7.3	10.0	13.2	18.5
Turkmenistan	992.4	83.7	16.8	24.2	8.3	11.6	8.8	5.6	5.9	10.7	10.5	9.0	12.0
Uzbekistan	54.0	70.9	29.0	29.1	25.0	27.3	27.3	11.6	6.6	10.0	14.2	12.3	11.8
Central Eastern Europe and the Baltic states													
Czech Republic	8.9	8.4	10.6	2.1	4.0	4.7	1.8	0.2	2.8	1.9	2.5	2.9	3.5
Estonia	23.1	11.2	8.1	3.3	4.0	5.8	3.6	1.3	3.0	4.1	4.4	6.6	9.6
Hungary	23.6	18.3	14.3	10.0	9.8	9.2	5.3	4.7	6.8	3.6	3.9	8.0	5.9
Latvia	25.0	17.6	8.4	4.7	2.4	2.5	1.9	2.9	6.2	6.7	6.5	10.1	14.3
Lithuania	24.6	8.9	5.1	0.8	1.0	1.5	0.3	-1.2	1.2	2.7	3.7	5.7	10.2
Poland	19.9	14.9	11.8	7.3	10.1	5.5	1.9	0.8	3.5	2.2	1.2	2.5	4.0
Slovak Republic	5.8	6.1	6.7	10.6	12.0	7.3	3.3	8.5	7.5	2.5	4.5	2.8	3.3
Slovenia	9.9	8.4	8.0	6.2	8.9	8.4	7.5	5.6	3.6	2.5	2.5	3.6	4.0
Bulgaria	123.0	1,082.0	22.2	0.7	9.9	7.4	5.9	2.3	6.1	5.0	7.3	8.4	10.9
Croatia	3.5	3.6	5.7	4.0	4.6	3.8	1.7	1.8	2.1	3.3	3.2	2.9	6.0
Romania	38.8	154.8	59.1	45.8	45.7	34.5	22.5	15.4	12.0	9.5	6.9	4.8	7.2
Median for Central Eastern Europe and Baltic states	23.1	11.2	8.4	4.7	8.9	5.8	3.3	2.3	3.6	3.3	3.9	4.8	6.0
Median for Post Soviet Countries	43.6	16.7	10.6	25.9	19.8	10.6	5.8	6.0	7.0	9.8	9.2	10.5	14.1
Average for Central Eastern and Baltic States	27.8	121.3	14.5	8.7	10.2	8.2	5.1	3.8	5.0	4.0	4.2	5.3	7.2
Average for Post-Soviet Countries	151.5	34.5	19.7	48.2	29.3	17.2	10.8	9.5	8.4	8.9	9.0	10.7	14.8

The source: EBRD

This kind of twofold situation tends to be created when in the conditions of abundant currency flow, in order to block inflation, delivery of the national currency is limited, which on one hand, strengthens the national currency and mitigates inflation, but on the other hand, for the purpose of ensuring stability of the currency rate, delivery of the national currency becomes necessary to be increased and this in turn, enhances the inflation growth.

Between these two contradictory actions, the selection in favor of either the prices or the stability of the exchange rate is being decided let's say, by choosing the "golden middle" in the countries with mixed monetary regimes, which means that along with relatively high inflation level, moderate strengthening of the exchange rate will also take place. Radical improvement of any of them will bring about worsening of the other.

Just as a coin has two sides, in the economy also, juxtaposed events as well as realization of economic goals are contradictory in character. The economy never develops in a linear direction and conflicts of interest often occur. It is well known to everyone that the goal of economic policy cannot be reduction of inflation and unemployment to happen simultaneously; it is impossible to increase the social expenditures with a background of reduced fiscal revenues; it's also impossible to strengthen the national currency and increase exports or reduce the income rates, etc., at one and the same time. One goal is achieved at the expense of another; it is impossible to achieve all the goals and objectives altogether, at one time and therefore, the unfulfilled goals are always exposed to criticism.

We must assume that in a country undergoing structural reforms, inflation grows and the exchange rate changes only in cases where the monetary policy is based on realization of the mixed goals.

Restriction of inflation by way of employing monetary instruments is rather limited. It should be supplemented by a strict fiscal policy and the remedies for optimization of the public expenditures. In the conditions of fast economic development, bilateral investments practiced by the Central Bank are limited and in fact, are directed to maintain the status quo.

In general, inflation as well as revaluation of national currencies represents a reflexive manifestation of the political remedies, whereas the monetary effect received by the change of the political course is related to implementation of the governmental policy.

All the above-mentioned implies that the process of deterioration of the financial-currency balance and its rehabilitation is empirically expressing the relationship of the government and the economic agents; the political, institutional and social-economic changes represent the expectations of the economic agents.

3.3. Political Economy of the Exchange Rate Regulations

The mentioned problem is studied in modern political literature based on the empiric data and the emphasis is on their peculiarities, on the results of operation of this policy as well as on the prices and the financial stability. Inflation control is one of the main problems of the economics of the post-communist countries. In effect of the price growth, the resources will be redistributed and new inflation expectancy will be developed. Forming of the market institutions as a result of post-privatization also had an impact on the price growth. The price growth was considerably ahead of forming the new market institutions and as a result of this, the market competition formed later on, proved unable to become a hindering factor in bridling the prices.

In the developed countries, the monetary policy is directed towards economic growth and reducing unemployment, whereas in the post-Soviet countries the vector is targeted to the price and financial stabilization, and certain transactional taxes should be paid by these countries because they embarked on this route. Instability of prices is accompanied by increase of prices on the financial assets which brings about movement of the capital from the real sector to the financial sector.

Thus, the capital is working not in favor of wellbeing but in the direction of increasing the speculative prices on the assets in the financial sector. As a result, investments keep decreasing in the real sector. In such conditions the economic activities as well as the monetary savings get decreased, too. The countries in question applied different methods for overcoming the above said problems but the main accent was on utilization of the monetary instruments and approbation of the regimes of the exchange rate.

In today's world there are a number of ongoing discussions with regard to the type of exchange regime appropriate to a country. This question is still unsettled among the economists and politicians because whatever is appropriate for one country proves unacceptable to another. Every country has its characteristic features and therefore, some of them managed to use efficiently different variations of the **fixed exchange rate** regime. It means that they "linked" their national currency to the currency of the country, with which they are in relations of priority integration. American dollar proved to be such a link to most of the countries whereas Euro was chosen by the EU member states, such as the Baltic countries, for instance. Hyperinflation as well as the unfavorable practice of financing by central banks of the government budget was a characteristic feature to such countries. For the purpose of escaping from such a situation and based on legislation, they established the fixed exchange rate.

In the situation when the exchange rate is fixed, the value of the currency will be transformed according to the change of the “anchor” exchange rate. For instance, if the USD is devaluated with regard to Euro, then the national currency of those countries which are linked with their currency to the USD will also be devaluated under the same proportion.

Introduction of the fixed exchange rate is the same as using the foreign competition for the purpose of stopping the price growth on the goods of local produce. Effectiveness of such policies depends on the ability of the producers to be extremely flexible in changing their prices as well as in delivery of the product.

The fixed exchange rate can influence the correlation of prices on those goods which are being sold at foreign markets. Such goods are the production facilities and the raw materials. Apart from this, when the expenditures on the work force get increased, the artificially suspended currency rate becomes the blocking factor for attracting foreign investments.

In the conditions of moderately high inflation and growth of the foreign investments, introduction of the fixed rate creates the illusion that the exchange rate of the national currency is stable against the other currencies, but instead, the probability of increase of the inflation grows higher because the pressure of the foreign currency and the investments over the economy will continue forth. The “Dutch illness” or the income which had not been generated by the economy of the country (and its source is the grants of non-economic character, as well as from foreign investments, privatization, export of the natural resources, etc.) will increase again the demand on conversion of the natural currency and as a result, its amount will keep growing in circulation, whereas objection to the measures of its sterilization will make the prices jump up even higher. This kind of a scenario may become characteristicof the oil and gas producing post-communist countries: Azerbaijan, Kasakhstan, Russia Turkmenistan. They are prone to the “Dutch illness”, because their main export products share in total exports is very high (from 55 percent in Russia to 90 percent in Azerbaijan).

By introducing the fixed course, the countries are objecting to developing their independent monetary system and thus become dependant on the policies imposed by the countries with the “anchor” currency. All this is painfully manifested in foreign trade.

In order to get necessary advantages, the governments use changes of the exchange rate and get engaged in “trade wars” against each other. This concerns big countries in particular. When the smaller countries get integrated with them, then by introducing the fixed currency regime they protect themselves from the "trade wars" and become part of the trade policy of the big countries.

It is well known that devaluation of the currency rate diminishes the export prices of the country and accordingly, increases the export prices. It is quite favorable for developing exports in the country, whereas strengthening of the currency rate makes the export prices grow, thus lessening the comparative price on imports. Local citizens buy the imported goods for cheaper prices and this situation is enhancing the development of imports whereas exports are decreasing.

In smaller countries, moderately high inflation commands active use of the monetary instruments and strengthening integration with the stable partner countries. Unlike the oil-producing countries, the small post-Soviet countries are approaching this problem in different ways.

In the underdeveloped economics shaky exchange rates are connected with high risk factors, but in the case of a fixed exchange rate, very often it becomes victim of speculative attacks.

The countries where different varieties of a fixed exchange rate are introduced (complete dollarization or a currency board), mostly belong to a group of small countries; these currency regimes are used by the rulers of the territories which are representatives of the separatist governments not recognized by the world community; therefore they are using the currency of their protector country. Such territories are the so-called Abkhazia and the South Ossetia (in Georgia) and the pre-Dnestrovye in Moldova.

Dollarization or a currency board is a reaction on the instability and high inflation rate in the country; it is a mechanism of self-defense and evading devaluation of the national currency which changes under the risk of devaluation of the foreign currency.

It is easier to put the currency board to operation. The countries, which are engaged in complete dollarization or Euroization, practically are excluding devaluation of the currency and this enhances reduction of interest rates because of lesser risks for decrease of exchange rate of foreign currency. Also, they are deprived of the opportunity of getting the income by seniorage despite the fact that the Currency board can extend such opportunities.

Dollarization and the currency board are supporting the economic integration with the country whose currency is recognized as a means of clearing. This is mostly manifested in integration of the banking system, but instead, the mentioned countries lose control over the monetary policy and if the risk of bank crisis emerges, the country won't have the opportunity to turn the Central Bank into the creditor of the national banking system and thus ensure its stability. This is why they fail to provide a normal functioning of the tax system. Therefore, the countries following the policies of the currency board are hardly able to implement it in a classical form.

Just as during one of the regimes of the fixed exchange rate, the money supply to the currency board depends on the state of balance of payment. For the minor and open economies, where such a regime exists, change in money delivery is defined mostly by the countries whose capital is invested in those countries. Therefore, the local financial policy becomes passive and the foreign capital starts to manage development of those countries. The dynamics of money delivery is determined by the production dynamics and the issuance is determined by the foreign companies and those financial flows, which are entering these countries from abroad. In this case, these are just the foreign investments which determine the development of the country. This is characteristic of the Baltic countries, because the relative contribution of the foreign investments in their GDP is high enough.

As studies have shown, the countries of the currency board, compared to other countries, hardly have a higher pace of GDP growth or a low level of inflation. There, the risk of speculative influence on behalf of the foreign investors is low and their integration with the currency of the mother country is strong enough.

As experts suggested, currency board could be very unflexible against the appreciation of national currency. In case of its introduction, it will be necessary, given the fixed exchange rate, to emit increasingly more currency, which will further accelerate the inflation; the foreign currency reserves, considering a country's scarce export potential will instantly deplete and become a cause of a deep financial crisis (Papava V., 2007. p. 8).

Currency board is the alternative for the Central Bank. It carries out conversion of a national currency at a fixed rate to a stable foreign currency or a currency basket without any restrictions in an automatic regime. This will require the country to have large amounts of foreign currency in order not to impede currency conversion operations at a fixed rate. The introduction of the Currency Board mechanism is expedient when there is a very high inflation rate in the country. During the currency board interest rates and inflation forms correspondingly of foreign country, whose currency serves as a shield in the exchange proceeds. In case of lack of international reserves and deterioration of export conditions, the country would not have the ability to pursue a relatively effective monetary policy and the risk of financial crisis occurs.

The targeted exchange rate policy is mostly carried out by the highly developed and institutionally well organized countries, whereas targeting of inflation and money delivery in the post-Soviet countries, because of the immature public institutions, fail to be always successful.

In the countries, where the economy is dollarizied, targeting of the exchange rate is one of the best options and it plays an essential role in reducing inflation, because the inflation effect of the national currency gets reduced (Sahay and Vegh, 1995). Apart from this, the fixed exchange rate has the effect of introducing order into the economy also in the case when the monetary as well as fiscal policy is not targeted at reducing inflation. But if the real rate of the national currency is increasing and the demand for the goods produced within the country gets reduced and the demand for the goods of foreign make keeps increasing, then a recession will be expected in such a country.

The fixed exchange rate has certain advantages on the initial stage of the transition period and therefore, using it for achieving macroeconomic stability is far more effective, but it only has a provisional character. Free exchange rate is an indicator of the corrections undertaken in the monetary policy which enhances regulation of the investment flow in the country. If the flow of capital causes the increase of bank deposits and an abundant flow of bank credits in the economy, then the use of the fixed exchange rate will cause an increase of the monetary resources and cause inflation, and later on, it will provoke emergence of risks and shocks in the financial system.

In order to operate the fixed exchange rate, existence of the currency reserves, strict fiscal discipline and independence of the monetary policy is a necessary precondition. In other cases, the fixed rate is unacceptable and targeting of the money delivery will become its alternative.

Targeting the money delivery as well as targeting the exchange rate is simple and transparent. It gives a clear signal on suspending inflation and thus reduces expectation of inflation. It is true that such a policy yielded a successful result in many countries, yet a number of experts have their doubts about this policy because of the following reasons: instability of money delivery is a characteristic feature of the post-communist countries and therefore, the link between the monetary aggregates and inflation is rather weak and targeting of the money delivery hardly yields any tangible outcome. Accordingly, it is impossible to carry out the disinflation policy quickly (De Broeck, Krajinyak, & Lorie, 1997; Wagner, 1998).

Under the assertions of some experts, in conditions of moderate inflation targeting of the money delivery requires the expenditures which are related to reduction of economic activities and a sharp increase of the interest rates (Sahay and Vegh, 1995).

During recent years, many countries have moved to t**argeted inflation**. This policy became wide-spread since the 90s and it is widely used in the developed countries. Use of this policy is rather attractive in the post-communist countries because the goal is clear enough. It also proved to be successful in many transition countries (The Czech Republic, Poland and Hungary).

In order to implement such a policy, a number of conditions have to be satisfied: the National Bank should be carrying out an independent policy and should strictly follow the targeted parameters. In addition to this, it should make accurate prognosis and undertake inflation control as well. With this in view, index of the consumer prices is used, although the negative side of this indicator is that its short-term quakes are no longer connected with the monetary policy. During implementation of such policies, it is necessary to ensure harmonious activities undertaken by the fiscal and monetary authorities, particularly in the expenditure part of the budget.

The countries, which follow targeting of inflation, would hardly reject the fact that their interim goal is to influence the money delivery or the real exchange rate of the national currency. The countries following the fixed exchange rate are setting before them an interim goal of either the real exchange rate of the national currency or creating international reserves. In the mentioned countries, the monetary policy is considerably dependant on the balance of payment or in other words, the monetary policy is not independent because of the fixed exchange rate of the national currency and because of peculiarities of the economy of these countries as well. The countries which hardly follow any regime at all are not consequential in determining their interim as well as final goals with regard to the monetary policy.

According to the ideas of certain experts (Wagner, 1998), on the initial stage of the transitional period, targeting of the money delivery or the exchange rate was quite appropriate. The countries which already went through this stage will have to move to the floating rate and establish the currency corridors or enhance change of the currency rate (crawing peg). Such a transition is appropriate to the advanced post-communist countries.

One of the characteristic features of the targeted exchange rate is that the central bank is unable to carry out the policy different from that of the country whose national currency represents an “anchor” currency to which it is tightly linked.

Different regimes of the exchange rate are a characteristic feature of the post-communist countries. According to some research studies, selection of the best exchange rate is related to the extent of trust in the investor and the competitive production characteristic to the world markets. In addition, it is of paramount importance to consider the liabilities taken with regard to the foreign currency (Calvo, 1999; Calvo and Reinhart, 2000; Calvo and Vegh, 1992). In the post-communist countries achieving stabilization by means of regulating the exchange rate is less efficient when inflation develops under inertia and the national currency has no credibility. This is why the experts, while selecting the regime of the exchange rate, are paying paramount attention to the interrelationship of flexibility and credibility (Edwards, 1996).

In the conditions of the **floating exchange rate**, for the purpose of influencing the exchange rate, the central banks will undertake interventions but in the times of the fixed exchange rate the economic agents believe that the central banks will maintain the exchange rate to at least some extent. The economic studies are mostly aimed at these two directions. In the conditions of a free exchange rate, the country is engaged in implementation of an independent financial policy and reacts to the interior as well as foreign shocks by way of changes of the trade conditions or of the interest rates. This kind of flexibility of the financial policy can be shaken by the trust of the foreign partners and it will give way to the expectation of inflation, whereas the fixed exchange rate reduces the flexibility of the policy, but instead, increases the credibility of the financial policy of the country; this will happen if there exists the belief that the central bank has enough reserves to maintain the exchange rate and the agents are capable of reducing the expectation of inflation.

Selection of a flexible and fixed exchange rate depends on the peculiarities of the development of the country. When there are monetary and political risks in a country, which are caused by foreign trade and a changeable disposition of the investors then use of the floating exchange rate is quite appropriate, but if the monetary policy being implemented in the country is unstable, then it is preferable to use the artificially fixed rate (at least for a short period of time) because the fundamental macroeconomic alterations and the foreign conditions will change quickly (Klaus, 1997).

According to the assertions of the floating course, this regime is effective for correction of the payment balance but an inconsistent exchange rate may create risks with regard to reducing the foreign investments. As a result, investments will be reduced whereas instability and inflation will grow.

In general, theoretical arguments pertaining to advantages of this or that exchange rate hardly give any opportunities for yielding correct recommendations, yet by means of empirical approaches those arguments are reflecting the risks and the positive results, which are characteristic to each of the rates mentioned above. The choice of the monetary regimes always takes place with regard to shocks but such a choice is problematic by itself.

In the dollarized countries, research studies assert that the change of the national currency on the dollar will bring about the growth of instability of the exchange rate. The floating exchange rate, along with the change of expectations, becomes rather sensitive. Free floating of the exchange rate will become the cause of reducing demand on the national currency (Berg and Borenstein, 2000). The flexible exchange rate acquires advantages when crises and shocks are dominating in the economy. Independent financial policy, a flexible exchange rate and a free movement of the capital are incompatible with each other, especially for the countries with weakly developed interior markets. In such countries, under the recommendation of the experts, a floating exchange rate should be introduced with very few restrictions over the movement of the capital, by maintaining autonomy of the monetary policy or the fixed exchange rate without the restrictions over the movement of the capital, but in exchange for losing autonomy of the monetary policy (Cooper, 1999).

According to the viewpoints established in the 90s, the fixed exchange rate as well as the floating rate yield equal results. In addition to this, according to some results already obtained, for instance, out of 28 developing countries with the fixed exchange rate, only a few of them had low inflation. Therefore, in most of the countries the fixed exchange rate proved to be ineffective for maintaining the low level of inflation (Little, Cooper, Corden and Rajapatirana, 1993). Also, a bigger part of the developing countries changed the fixed exchange rate and moved to the flexible exchange rates.[‡‡]

The lessons learned are the following: the post-communist countries with the budgets with little deficit, are trying to establish a strict exchange rate regime in the conditions of "open economy". The countries which are trying to correct the exchange rate in the conditions of a fixed exchange rate would experience lower inflation rather than if they adopted the floating exchange rate. If while moving to the new exchange rate regime, the macroeconomic indicators don't demand the alterations of the exchange rate regime, the inflation pace will change but only slightly.

When the inflation tempo is insignificant, flexibility of the exchange rate should keep growing in order to maintain the competitive capacity of the country, but in the conditions of a high inflation pace the exchange rate regime should be strict in order to take the role of the "anchor" which would hold inflation.

Today, an option between the floating and fixed exchange rates is regarded as the option between trust and flexibility. The floating exchange rate is effective for correcting the payment balance. Ambiguity of the currency rate increases the risks

‡‡ Among them Argentina, some African countries etc.

for foreign investments and this is why instability sets in. Yet instability is one of the most important problems for the post-communist countries because of which they are moving to the strict exchange rate regime. They declare their objectives and aspirations in order to lessen ambiguity and the inflation risks. Increase of the international reserves is the outcome of this situation (see Table 8). After the currency crisis of 1998–1999, the international reserves, for the purpose of neutralizing the expected speculative attacks against the currency market acquired a greater significance. The "mercantile" policy of this sort demands a continuous increase of the reserves, which in turn, strengthens inflation and gives power to the national currency. By this action, the central banks of the countries in question, because of devaluation of their main currency reserve (the USD), are losing their income. The stable exchange rate in the conditions of macroeconomic stability will give stimulus to the de-dollarization of the economy.

The regime of the fixed exchange rate is lessening flexibility of the policy but is increasing the credibility of the policy which is ensuring stability and low pace of inflation. Such a policy will only be justified if the economic agents are trusting the government in providing stability; therefore, there are recommendations that the fixed exchange rate regime should be adjusted to the measures taken for the purpose of increasing confidence among the economic agents (Drobiyshevskaya et al., 2003. p.67).

Therefore, it can be concluded that openness of the economy is a determining factor in selecting the currency regime. If the main goal of the country is attracting foreign capital and building economy, then the fixed rate regimes will enhance fulfillment of this goal, but if the country is extending efforts to establish itself on the world markets, then the financial policy should support development of the national economy and at this point the floating exchange rate will yield positive results. When the country is willing to ensure both variants, then it should play a game that may turn rather risky as well. If at the background of the fixed exchange rate, the release defines the dynamics of delivery, in the conditions of the targeted inflation this process will be going the other way round.

Thus, inflation is one more goal which shows up in the monetary policy and is working in an entirely opposite direction than the exchange rate regime. In such conditions, the price shocks are already influencing the release and the expectations of inflation would enhance increase of instability.

In the transition countries, use of the financial instruments mostly depends on either the foreign trade relations or on attraction of foreign investments. Big countries mostly use the channels of bank crediting and the currency rates. In the countries with targeted inflation, the bank crediting channels are given priority.

This situation is verifying the necessity of conducting a balanced policy by the central bank.

Table 8. International reserves (Except gold, in USD, by the end of the year)

	1996	1997	1998	1999	2000	2001	2002	2003	2004	2005	2006	2006/1996
Azerbaijan	214	467	447	673	680	725	721	803	1,075	1,178	2,500	11.7
Byelorussia	469	394	703	294	350	391	417	462	691	1,107	1,069	2.3
Estonia	703	821	876	944	921	820	1,000	1,373	1,793	1,945	2,856	4.1
Latvia	622	704	728	840	851	1,149	1,241	1,432	1,912	2,232	4,353	7.0
Lithuania	834	1,063	1,460	1,242	1,359	1,669	2,413	3,450	3,594	3,816	5,773	6.9
Moldova	312	366	144	186	222	229	269	302	470	597	775	2.5
Russia	11,276	12,895	7,801	8,457	24,264	32,542	44,054	73,175	120,809	175,900	295,568	26.2
Georgia	158	173	118	132	109	161	198	191	383	474	881	5.6
Armenia	156	229	281	291	302	317	416	502	548	669	1,072	6.9
Tajikistan	14	30	65	58	87	96	96	135	189	235	252	18.0
Turkmenistan	1,172	1,285	1,379	1,555	1,808	2,055	2,346	2,673	2,714	3,442	5,425	4.6
Ukraine	1,960	2,341	761	1,046	1,353	2,955	4,241	6,731	9,302	19,413	22,300	11.4
Uzbekistan	772	374	533	763	684	1,212	1,215	1,659	2,146	2,895	4,665	6.0
Kazakhstan	1,295	1,697	1,461	1,479	1,594	1,997	2,555	4,962	9,277	7,070	19,113	14.8
Kyrgyzstan	95	170	164	230	205	230	289	365	549	570	764	8.1

The source: EBRD

Despite diverse currency-financial regimes different from each other, the countries are still implementing various interim goals which may be the following: in the currency board countries — targeted inflation; in the currency board countries as well as in the countries of targeted inflation — real exchange rate; in the countries of almost all regimes — targeting of the international reserves and the monetary aggregates.

In the countries of open economy, especially in smaller countries, the dependence on the foreign shocks is too great and if these countries follow targeted inflation or the money supply then such dependence will be even greater. Despite this, they have a vast area of monetary instruments to neutralize this situation. In addition to this, they are less prone to the speculative attacks of the foreign investors. In such cases, contribution of the interior savings should be high enough in order to be able to increase the competitiveness of the national economy.

In the countries with the fixed exchange rate regime the monetary dynamics is preconditioned by economic production. They depend on the financial and economic integration with the main trading countries and they are almost deprived of the instruments that would secure them from the foreign shocks.

The countries, which connect implementation of their currency policy with the partner countries are following the fixed exchange rate regimes and by this, they lose the opportunity of crediting the banking system by means of the income obtained from seniorage because the financial risks are increasing and are unable to ensure their neutralization, whereas the countries which are engaged in implementation of flexible financial policy, become significantly dependant on the joint policy of the central bank and the government, as well as on the prognosis of the parameters and the unexpected risks. In these countries, too, probability of the financial crisis is high enough.

Eventually, the answer to the question: which monetary regime should be chosen by the country in order to enhance growth of the economy and stability will depend on several factors: 1. Trust in the government; 2. Aspiration of foreign investments to enter the national market; 3. Competitiveness of local production; 4. Macroeconomic situation in the country. It is for the mentioned directions that the monetary policy of the country can be defined.

CONCLUSION

Financial instability, expectancy of state interventions in the economy, speculative pressures for the purpose of getting profits, etc., represent preconditions of emergence of the risks in financial regulation. All the agents, the state, the business community and the civil society are participants in this economic game. All of them have their own interests and the quintessence of it is an aspiration towards the stability and growth of financial income in the currency of the country which is capable of realizing the mentioned goals. Speculative attacks of the economic agents against the national currency and the inadequate reaction of the government to it are acting as the stimulators of the crises in these relations which are a reflective image of the existing economic situation. These relations are developing according to various scenarios.

When the civil society is expecting a worsening of the economic situation then they take relevant precautions against the national currency, and the economic situation of the country will be getting worse indeed.

The government will face the necessity of making a compromise in an option of employing the proper methods for maintaining the best exchange rate: either the short-term flexibility or gaining a long-term credibility. The crisis starts when it turns out that it is more costly to keep the existing parity and also with the belief that keeping the existing balance in the marker is ineffective. Speculative pressure over the currency emerges in the course of the expectancy of worsening of the economic situation. Relevantly, it should be concluded that a weak financial system gives way to the belief of instability and the economic balance will become more deteriorated.

The financial risks are caused by bad banking management, corporative problems and the micro- and macroeconomic results of all this. The capital flows and incorrect investments precondition devaluation of the currency, which in turn is weakening the financial-banking sector and real economy. Weakness of the real economy bears pessimistic expectations among the investors and these expectations will enhance ousting of the financial flows from the country even more.

According to the experience of the countries, incorrect economic policy always gives birth to the pessimistic expectations of the economic agents. The financial market gives an acute reaction to each, even insignificant changes in politics. It can take negative actions but the initial reasons for the irregularities are always connected with the behavior of the government.

In all countries, assessment of the currency policy and its diagnostics (although they are not developing according to the same scenario and are exquisitely peculiar) is based on the system of indicators, which represents the unity of financial-banking, macroeconomic, social, institutional and political factors. The mentioned system of indicators is universal and the economic, financial and social situation manifested by each of them acquires different meanings in all countries, and reaction to it is a precondition for prevention of disproportion.

In the post-Soviet countries of the 90s, the widespread financial-currency crises revealed the weaknesses of transformation and low effectiveness of the reforms. It is true, that Georgia, Moldova, Kyrgyzstan and Kazakhstan were considered to be the leaders of transformation but the programs for transformation proved to be inefficient and insufficient for escaping the crisis. The tax problems and financial irregularities of the countries are still pending as enhancing circumstances to the mentioned crises, whereas ineffectiveness of the social programs had an impact on making the inflation deeper.

In the countries, where the social-economic reforms were not expedited, the delay was caused by the deficit of the political consensus. In addition, political instability and unresolved ethno-conflicts make the opportunities for stabilization even more complicated. The investors refrain from investing their capital in such countries, because of the suspicious results that it may yield. All this is creating the conditions for destroying the financial balance in economically weak and ethnically unsettled countries because this can be done easily enough there.

Dwelling on this, it can be noted that a periodical deterioration of the financial-currency balance is a characteristic feature of the post-communist countries; it is true that it hardly has a strict character but it gives stimulus to the investments that the government and the central bank undertake at the financial-currency markets and together with the financial balance, strengthens the risks as well.

It is hard to say what kind of results such "games" will yield. A lot of things depend on the confidence that the public will grant to the government.

REFERENCES

[1] Andreou I., Dufrénot G., Sand-Zantman A., & Zdzienicka-Durand A. (2007). A Forewarning indicator System for Financial crises: *The case of six Central and Eastern European countries. Working Paper, no 901, May*. William Davidson Institute. Available from: http://www.wdi.umich.edu/files/Publications/WorkingPapers/wp901.pdf

[2] Antczak, R. (2000). *Theoretical Aspects of Currency Crises*. Warsaw: Center for Social and Economic Research.

[3] Berg A., & Borenstein, E.(2000). The Choice of Exchange Rate Regime and Monetary Target in Highly Dollarized Economies. *Working paper, no 29. IMF*.

[4] Bokros, L. (2001). Experience and Perspectives of Financial sector Development in Central and Eastern Europe. *Working paper Series, no 38*. Warsaw: Center For Social and Economic Research.

[5] Blaszkewicz M. (2000). What factors led to the Asian Financial Crisis: Were or were not Asian Econcmics Sound? Warsaw: Center For Social and Economic Research.

[6] Calvo G. (1999). Fixed versus Flexible Exchange Rate: Preliminaries of a Turnof Millennium Rematch. Available from: *www.bsos.umd.edu/econ /ciecalvo.htm.*

[7] Calvo G., & Reinhart C. (2000). Fear of Floating. University of Maryland.

[8] Calvo G., & Vegh C. (1992). Inflation Stabilization and Nominal Anchors. *Working paper, 92/4. IMF.*

[9] Cooper, R. (1999). Exchange Rate Choices, mimeo. Harvard University.

[10] Dabrowski, M. (ed). (2001). *Currency Crises in Emerging Markets - Selected Comparative*. Warsaw: Center For Social and Economic Research.

[11] Dabrowski, M.,& Gortat R.(2002). Political Determinant of economic Reforms in Former Comunist Countries. *Studies and Analysis. no 242.* Warsaw: Center For Social and Economic Research.

[12] De Broeck, M., Krajinyak K., & Lorie H. (1997). Explaning and Forecasting the Velocity of Money in Transition Economies, with Special Reference to the Baltics, Russia and other Countries of the Soviet Union. *Working paper, 97/108*. IMF.

[13] *Discussion Papers, no, 2*, Bank of Finland, Institute for Economies in Transition.

[14] Dombrovski M. (1999). *Posledstvyia Rosi'skogo finansovogo krisisa dlyia sosedskix stran*. Warsaw: Center For Social and Economic Research.

[15] Drobiyshevskaya C., et. all. (2003). Sravnitel'ni' analiz denejno-kreditnoi' politiki v perexodnyix ekonomyikax. *Working Paper no 58P*. Moscow: Institute of Economics of transitional period,

[16] Edwards, S. (1996). The Determinants of the Choice Between Fixed and Flexible Exchange – Rate Regimes *Working paper, 5756*. NBER

[17] ERBRD. Available from: http://www.ebrd.com/country/sector/econo/stats/sei.xis

[18] Fisher S., & Sahay R.(2000). The Transition Economies After Ten Years. *Working Paper WP/00/30* (February 1). IMF. Availabe from: *www.imf.org/external/pubs/ft/wp.2000/wp0030.pdf*

[19] Gaidar E. (2004). Social'no-economicheskaya transformatsya v stranax SNG: dostijenya i problemy. In E. Gaidar (ed), "*Post communist transformation in CIS countries: Achievements and problems", (p.9-10),* Moscow: Institute of Economics of Transitional Period.

[20] Jarocinski M. (1998). Money Demand and Monetization in Transition Economies. *Working papers series, no 13.* Warsaw: Center For Social and Economic Research.

[21] Kakulia M. (2001). Problems of currency system development in Georgia, Tbilisi. (in Georgia).

[22] Kaminsky, G., Lizondo, S., Reinhart, C. (1998). *Leading Indicators of Currency Crises. Staff Papers, Vol. 45 # 1,* (March). IMF.

[23] Kazmer D., & Konrad M.(2005). *Economic Lessons frpm the Transition. The Basic Theory Re-exemined.*. Armonk, New York, London, England. M.E.Sharpe.

[24] Klaus V.(1997). Promoting Financial Stability in the Transition Economies of Central Eastern Europe. *Federal Reserve Bank of Kansas City.*

[25] Korhonen I., Wachtel P. (2005). A note on exchange rate pass-through in CIS countries.

[26] Lavigue, M. (2000). The Economics of the Transition Process. What have we learned? *Problems of Post-Communsm. July-August. Vol 47.* no 4. pp.16-24.

[27] Little I., Cooper R., Corden W, & Rajapatirana S. (1993). *Boom, Crisis and Adjustment. The Macroeconomic Experience of Developing Countries.* Oxford University Press for the World Bank.

[28] Papava, V. (2005a). *Macroeconomics of Post-communist transition period.* Tbilisi: Tbilisi State University Press. (in Georgia)

[29] Papava V.(2007). Currency Board Against the Background of Dutch Disease. *Georgian Economic Trends,* October, 2003. p. 8-10.

[30] Papava V. Chocheli V.(2003). *Financial Globalization and post-communist Georgia.* New York, Lincoln Shanghai. Universe, Inc.

[31] Papava V.(2005b). Necroeconomics. *The Political Economy of Post-communist Capitalism.* (Lessons from Georgia). New York Lincoln Shangai. iUniversal Inc.

[32] Radelet S., & Sachs J.(1998). *The East Asian Financial Crisis: Diagnosis, Remedies, prospects.* Harvard Institute for International Development. Available from: *http://www.stern.nyu.edu/-nrubina/asia*

[33] Sahay R, & Vegh C.(1995). Dollarization in transition economies: Evidence and policy implication., *Working paper, 95/96.* IMF

[34] Stiglitz J.(1998). The Role of International Finantial Institutions in the Current Global Economy. Address to the Chicago Council on Foreign Relations, February, 27, Chicago. *Available from: http://www.worldbank.org/html/extme/jssp022798.html*;

[35] Stiglitz, J.(1997). Interview in "Transition Economy Is still a Well-defined Category," Transition 8, no.6 (December). Availabel from: *www.worldbank.org/html/prddr/trans/pdf/novdec97.pdf*

[36] Tomczynzka M.(2000). *Early Indicators of Currency Crises. Review of some Literature.* Warsaw: Center For Social and Economic Research.

[37] UN statistic database. Available from:

[38] UNECE (2000). United Nations Economic Comission for Europe UNECE, *Economic Survey of Europe, Vol.1,* New York.
Useful Sources:

[39] Wagner H. (1998). Central Banking in Transition Countries. *Working paper, 98/126.* IMF.

[40] World Bank (2002). The first Ten Years: Analysis and Lessons for Eastern Europe and the Former Soviet Union. Report, no 23511, Available from: *http://wbln0018.worldbank.org/eca/eca.nsf*

[41] World Development Report. (1997). *The State in a Changing World*. World Bank. Oxford University Press.
[42] World Bank (2002a*). Transition, January-February.*
[43] World Bank (1998). *Transformation, June*, issue 9, no 3. *http:/unstats.un.org/unsd/snaama/selectionbasicFast.asp*
[44] World Economic Outlook Database. (2007). Available from: *www.imf.org/external/pubs/ft/weo/2007/01/data/index.aspx*
[45] World Development Indicators. Available from: *http://web.worldbank.org/WBSITE/EXTERNAL/DATASTATISTICS/*

INDEX

A

B

C

D

E

F

K

L

M

N

O

P

R

S

T

U

V

W

Y